What Experts

"This is a captivating glimpse into the world of senior living. Jill's examples and stories from her own work and personal experiences help us to understand that we alone don't have the answers, that we need to ask the people living and working in our communities. This book is honest and authentic and should be a must-read for anyone working or interested in the area of senior living."

Penny Cook, President and CEO, Pioneer Network

"Jill Vitale-Aussem's perspective on aging is profound and timely! Her ability to blend insights from her own experiences, leadership theory, and philosophies on successful aging make [this book] a read that needs to be on our bookshelves."

Michele Holleran, Ph.D., M.B.A., CEO and Founder, Holleran, and Former Chair, Larry Minnix LeadingAge Leadership Academy

"Filled with honesty and wit, Jill Vitale-Aussem holds up the mirror and takes us on her journey as a self-reflective leader as she grows from a successful master of hospitality into a genuine community builder and social architect. She helps us understand why this fundamental shift is vital to the well-being of elders . . . [and] equips the field of senior living with an arsenal of resources to drive a deep transformation of culture and build inclusive communities everywhere."

Jennifer Carson, Ph.D., Director, Dementia Engagement, Education and Research Program, School of Community Health Services, University of Nevada

"This is a great book that connects the dots between the isms of aging, the essential human components of living that we have often neglected in the systems we have developed, and where we need to go to better support each other as we grow older. It is filled with so many of my favorite things on these topics: the importance of community, authenticity, humility, and paradigm shifting, with a wealth of different perspectives, engaging stories, and practical examples."

Sonya Barsness, M.S.G., Revisionary Gerontologist, www.beingheard.blog

"Through real life stories and researched examples, Vitale-Aussem challenges our thinking about meeting the needs of older adults. From inviting us to reconsider the role of hospitality in our field, to a thorough exploration of surplus safety, I applaud Vitale-Aussem for raising such important issues."

Kirsten Jacobs, M.S.W., Director of Dementia and Wellness Education, LeadingAge

DISRUPTING THE STATUS QUO OF SENIOR LIVING

A MINDSHIFT

DISRUPTING THE STATUS QUO OF SENIOR LIVING

A MINDSHIFT

by

Jill Vitale-Aussem, MMH, LNHA

Baltimore • London • Sydney

Health Professions Press, Inc.
Post Office Box 10624
Baltimore, Maryland 21285-0624

www.healthpropress.com

Interior design by Erin Geoghegan. Cover design by Mindy Dunn.
Typeset by Absolute Service, Inc., Towson, MD.
Manufactured in the United States of America by Integrated Books International, Dulles, VA.

The names of senior living residents in this book have been changed to respect their privacy.

Photo on dedication page, credit to Eric Jones. Copyright © Christian Living Communities.

A range of AARP print and e-books are available at AARP's online bookstore, aarp.org/bookstore, and through local and online bookstores.

For information on additional resources for senior living and long-term care professionals, visit HPP's website at www.healthpropress.com.

Library of Congress Cataloging-in-Publication Data

Names: Vitale-Aussem, Jill, author.
Title: Disrupting the status quo of senior living : a mindshift / by Jill Vitale-Aussem, MMH.
Description: Baltimore : Health Professions Press, [2019] | Includes bibliographical references and index.
Identifiers: LCCN 2019001112 (print) | LCCN 2019004555 (ebook) | ISBN 9781938870842 (epub) | ISBN 9781938870828 (pbk.)
Subjects: LCSH: Older people--Care. | Life care communities--Management.
Classification: LCC HV1451 (ebook) | LCC HV1451 .V58135 2019 (print) | DDC 362.61--dc23
LC record available at https://lccn.loc.gov/2019001112

British Library Cataloguing in Publication data are available from the British Library.

Contents

This is for you, Mom and Dad.

About the Author

Jill Vitale-Aussem, MMH, LNHA, is a veteran of the senior living field with more than two decades of experience leading senior living communities in the for-profit and not-for profit sectors. Since 2018, she has served as President and CEO of The Eden Alternative, a global non-profit dedicated to creating quality of life for elders and their care partners, wherever they may live.

Vitale-Aussem earned a Master of Management in Hospitality from Cornell University School of Hotel Administration. She is a licensed nursing home administrator, a certified assisted living administrator, a LeadingAge Leadership Academy Fellow, an Eden Alternative Guide, and a Certified Eden Alternative Educator.

Vitale-Aussem is passionate about creating community cultures of innovation, possibilities, inclusivity, growth, and empowerment. She writes and speaks internationally on the topics of culture, leadership, and ageism.

Acknowledgments

Writing a book is both harder and more rewarding than I could have imagined. While much of the process of writing is spent in isolation, a book is the compilation of the experiences we've had and the people we've been lucky enough to learn from in our lives. It's impossible to name everyone who has influenced this book, but I'm deeply grateful to the following people and organizations.

I grew and learned from every community and organization I worked for over the years. The residents and team members whose stories and experiences I share, from my recollection of events and conversations as they occurred, are integral to the book and to important lessons I've learned.

The residents and team members of Clermont Park Life Plan Community taught me how to create a real community and provided me with a once-in-a-lifetime leadership opportunity. Clermont Park's parent organization, Christian Living Communities, gave me the freedom and encouragement to stretch further than I ever thought possible and allowed me to share in this book the story of our journey together.

Many architects, designers, professionals, and thought leaders named throughout this book generously shared their time, insights, and knowledge with me. I learned so much from each of them.

Many organizations have inspired me to think differently about aging, leadership, and myself. Most influential among these are The Eden Alternative, the organization that transformed my career and my life; Masterpiece Living, an organization that's teaching people how to live not just longer, but better; and the LeadingAge Leadership Academy, especially the Change Agents: Katherine Streeter, Nikole Jay, Debbie Hedges, Thomas Chang, Ilana Springer, Chris Sintros, Alla Rubenstein, and our coach Tama Carey.

I began exploring many of the topics in this book by blogging and writing articles for The Eden Alternative, *LeadingAge Magazine*, and ChangingAging.org. These publications gave me a voice and helped me feel comfortable in sharing my ideas and thoughts with our field.

Al Power, Roger Landry, and Nancy Fox all shared with me their own experiences as published authors and encouraged me to move ahead with my dream of writing a book.

AARP and its Books Director Jodi Lipson, in collaboration with Health Professions Press and its team, including Mary Magnus and Cecilia González, have the distinction of making this book a reality.

Many folks invested precious time reading the manuscript and providing valuable feedback: Janice Vitale, Mark Vitale, Laura Beck, Carly Andrews (who also helped me to refine my thoughts on the role of hospitality in the field), Katherine Streeter, Carli Lindemann, Pam Sullivan, and, of course, my parents, who promptly predicted it would be an international best seller.

My family participated in this project in so many ways. My mom and dad willingly shared their experiences as residents of a senior living community and propped me up with words of encouragement along the way. My sister, Janice, was incredibly supportive and spent countless hours reading this book and providing honest feedback and ideas. My brother, Mark, sister-in-law, Shawna, and nephews, Pete and Isaac, not only supported me but also reminded me to have fun during this journey.

Last, but not least, the guy who lives up to his last name every single day, my husband, Todd Aussem, has my deepest gratitude. You never doubted for a minute I could do it. And eventually I believed you.

Introduction

I'VE BEEN WORKING in the senior living field for many years, starting with a part-time job in a nursing home when I was 16 years old. Like most nursing homes in the mid-1980s, where I worked wasn't an especially welcoming place. The hallways were long and the floors were shiny. The building echoed with the sounds of carts rolling over tile. Slumped-over residents lined the hallways. The lighting, like the culture, was cold.

In the mid-1980s, most nursing homes were highly efficient, sterile, and clinical environments. The lives of residents were regimented and inflexible. Bedtimes, wake-up times, and meal times were dictated by staff. Nurses were trained on how to properly tie residents to their wheelchairs, and how to secure the wheelchairs to the handrails in the hallway to keep people from going where they shouldn't.

I was a dietary aide. Whether it was the result of my own shortcomings, or the environment I was working in, I wasn't engaged in my work or with the residents. I wasn't expected to be. The kitchen was set up like an assembly line, and I functioned like a factory worker. My job was to do as I was told and complete tasks as quickly as possible.

After school for a couple days each week, I would walk to the nursing home, enter through the back door of the kitchen, clock in, don my hairnet and gloves, and get to work. While the cook prepared the food, I would start setting up the tray line—a then common method of distributing food. I would line up rows of plastic trays and, on each one, place a tray card indicating each resident's dietary needs. The tray card was my bible, telling me what type of dishes, adaptive equipment, food texture, and drinks to place on each tray. No deviations were allowed.

There were no cooked-to-order options at this home. There was no menu to choose from. There were no choices at all. Residents ate what was on the menu, and that was that. Not even our beverage service offered any variety or choice. Based on historical preferences (which were usually discovered during admission to the nursing home), each resident received the same drink on his or her tray each night. If you said you liked milk and cranberry juice on the day you moved in, that's what you got. Every single day.

As dictated by the tray card, I would place feeding syringes on many trays. The syringes looked like the turkey baster my mom had in the kitchen at home—a long, graduated, plastic tube with a rubber bulb at the end. This is how residents needing a pureed diet were fed. The nurse's aide would squeeze the bulb to suck up the pureed mixture from a bowl and would then place the end of the syringe in the resident's mouth and squeeze again, injecting the goop into the resident's mouth. I recall setting a high percentage of trays with those turkey basters, though certainly nowhere near that number of people could have actually needed a pureed diet. I now understand the reason—it was much more efficient to squirt food into someone's mouth than to help the person eat with a fork or spoon.

The pureed food, at least in this nursing home, was made by throwing every menu item together in a blender. When the blender blades stopped whirring, the result was a steaming gelatinous mass. It was disgusting, no matter what the ingredients. But some combinations were positively unthinkable.

I'll never forget one evening in particular. On the stove sat a huge pot of steaming chicken noodle soup. Nearby, on the counter, was a pile of peanut butter and grape jelly sandwiches. I watched in disbelief as the cook threw it all in the blender together. Three decades have passed, but I can still smell that awful odor. I had to fight the gagging sensation of nausea as I ladled the thick gray glop into plastic bowls.

After the food was dished up, I would slide the trays onto shelves in a metal cart. An aide would then roll the cart to the dining room where a tray was plopped in front of each resident. It was the epitome of efficiency. And it was institutional dining at its worst—dehumanizing and degrading.

Once dinner was over, I'd wash the dishes and mop the floors, then clock out and walk home. As I passed the building, I could see through the windows into residents' rooms. Most residents were sitting and staring, seemingly at nothing. I remember thinking that this would be a miserable way to live. And I'm guessing for most of those elders, it was.

You're probably thinking this was a terrible place. It wasn't—at least according to the standards of the mid-1980s. Back then, there was little, if any, focus on choice or quality of life. A colleague of mine was a nursing assistant in a different home in a different state during that time period. She recalls the same dining practices and tells disturbing stories of forced enemas and barbaric wound care protocols. Back then there weren't assisted living or independent living communities or the wide range of options for care at home that we have today. If you couldn't live alone independently, this is where you ended up.

Thankfully, we've made progress. The image of gray goop being squeezed into mouths from a turkey baster is a far cry from the dining experiences being created today. Many new nursing homes and assisted and independent living communities offer fine dining experiences full of choices and restaurant-style service. Instead of rigid dining times, some communities offer open dining from morning to night. Pureed food is often prepared by emulsifying each individual item and then reshaping it in the appearance of the original food item. I've tried this improved version of pureed food. Other than the strange consistency, it's actually pretty good.

Outside the kitchen, things have changed as well. There are a multitude of living options. Newer communities may feel a bit more like home or have a resort-style look and feel. We don't force enemas or tie people to their wheelchairs anymore. Linoleum flooring, intercom systems, and noisy nurse call systems are, at least in newer buildings, gone. Lighting and the interior finishes are often warm and welcoming. Some higher-end communities offer appealing amenities, such as theaters, swimming pools, fitness centers, outdoor pizza ovens, bistros, and self-service beer kegs.

Unfortunately, while we may look different on the outside, deep inside, in our thought processes and systems, remnants of that old culture remain. Even in these beautiful new buildings, I've experienced cultures full of loneliness, helplessness, and boredom where few opportunities for growth, inclusion, and purpose exist. As Masterpiece Living's Roger Landry, M.D., an expert in successful aging, says: "We've made progress, but we're still missing critical pieces. There's a deep transformation in our thinking and beliefs that has yet to take place."

In 2018, the U.S. senior housing penetration rate (which refers to the total senior housing inventory divided by the number of people over the age of 80), stands at just under 12 percent and is projected to rise to only 12.5 percent in 2025.[1] Staying in one's home and remaining "independent" is an appealing concept to many. Multiple studies have found that most baby boomers want to age in place and, according to a 2018 AARP survey, 76 percent of Americans over the age of 50 plan to stay put in their homes as they age.[2] Many businesses have sprung up to support this wish. If you do an Internet search of "aging in place," you'll get thousands of results for home care agencies, transportation companies, home remodeling specialists, and other organizations that specialize in helping people stay in their homes as they get older.

Remaining at home is indeed a good option for some people. My grandmother thrived at home until she died at the age of 92. With the right physical environment and access to services and social support, people can age in place very successfully. Newer options, such as cohousing communities, intergenerational housing, and naturally occurring retirement communities (NORCs), are promising solutions that combine the privacy of home with the strength and support of a cohesive community.

Unfortunately, many older adults live in environments that *aren't* well suited to meet their needs. Gerontology professor Stephen M. Golant at the University of Florida goes so far as to say that these folks are not so much aging in place as rotting in place.[3]

The dissolution of traditional neighborhoods and the lack of a true sense of community in many parts of our country have led to a sad reality where social support, beyond the provision of basic services, often isn't available. In these situations, people may become isolated when they stay in the homes that they've inhabited for decades.

Neighbors and friends move or pass away. The neighborhood changes. People begin having health and mobility challenges, and it becomes harder and harder to get out into the world. This isolation often leads to depression, health issues, cognitive decline,[4] and even reduced life spans.[5] Research studies show these outcomes time and time again. In short, being cut off from the world begins the cycle of "circling the drain" that is extremely hard to reverse.

And while there is talk about technology as a means of keeping people engaged while staying in their homes, technology alone may not be the panacea we hope for. A study published in the *Journal of the American Geriatrics Society* found that older adults who have little face-to-face contact with others have almost twice the risk of developing depression.[6] While social media platforms were not part of the research, email and telephone contact was studied and did not reduce this risk. Other studies have found mixed results from the use of social media, with some finding that the use among older adults reduced isolation and others finding no impact or even an increase in loneliness.[7]

What it boils down to, in my opinion, is that congregate living environments are, and will continue to be, an important option for older adults. Yet many people, turned off by the image and status quo of senior living, stay in their homes and are determined to age in place, even when they live in less-than-optimal circumstances.

What is it about these communities that turns people off so much that they would rather wither away alone than make a change?

I believe it's partly the ageism that exists in our society (people don't want to admit they're old and don't want to live with old people), but also the institutional culture that persists, in every level of living and in even the most beautiful of buildings. It's a culture that purports to honor aging but continues, in many situations, to operate based on processes and policies infused with paternalism, ageism, and antiquated thinking.

My parents had always planned to remain in their home. It seemed like they had it all figured out. They were both avid hikers and fitness enthusiasts. They had lots of friends. They traveled the world. They'd also done an amazing job with their financial planning for retirement.

Things began to change when my mom began losing her vision due to retinitis pigmentosa, an incurable, irreversible retinal disease. My parents loved their home with its beautiful backyard and garden, and like most people, they wanted to stay put. They took steps to compensate for my mom's vision loss, adding new lighting and other adaptations to their house. It worked for a while but, unfortunately, as my mom's vision loss progressed, she became more and more dependent on my dad.

This new reality didn't sit well with my mom, who had long held the fitting nickname, Marge-in-Charge. As she lost her fiercely held independence, she experienced deep frustration, anger, and sadness. She began to lose confidence in her ability to get out on her own, and my siblings and I started seeing the early signs of helplessness and disengagement from the world. At the same time, we noticed our dad struggling under immense levels of stress as he tried to support our mom.

In their small town, there was no nearby cohousing community or NORC. And support options, beyond basic home care services, were virtually nonexistent. Much as they wanted to stay in their home with the beautiful backyard, they realized it just wouldn't work.

We knew that living in a community setting would help both my mom and my dad, but they resisted for a time, fearful of living in an institutional setting and losing control over their own lives.

Eventually, they found a community that embodies many of the innovative ideas and practices that we'll discuss in this book. They're now happy and engaged in life, and my mom has regained her spirit and independence. And, interestingly, while the main reason for the move was to provide more opportunities for my mom, my dad is benefitting as much as she is from this new living environment.

How can we make congregate living settings a more compelling option when staying at home isn't the answer? How can we make independent living communities, assisted living communities, and nursing homes better places to live?

I had the great fortune to work for Christian Living Communities, a senior living organization in Denver, Colorado, that encouraged me to challenge the status quo and create something different. My first job with the organization was as executive director at Clermont Park Life Plan Community, which offers independent, assisted, and memory support living as well as a nursing home and adult day programming. When I started, the community was on the cusp of an $80 million redevelopment project that would replace the tired and institutional framework and physical plant with a vibrant new building. It was designed to house a culture of possibilities, growth, and innovation and to bring together into one inclusive community older adults with different care needs and socioeconomic backgrounds.

It was my job to drive the cultural transformation that would match that building. Inspired by the principles and philosophy of The Eden Alternative (an international not-for-profit organization dedicated to improving the life of elders and their care partners wherever they may live), we tinkered, we experimented, we pushed the envelope, and we made many, many mistakes. But together, the people who lived and worked in that community created something spectacular and achieved things we never thought possible. We shifted from the traditional framework of segregation, paternalistic rules, and institutional mindsets to an inclusive culture of possibilities and purpose, where people continued to grow and flourish, instead of just existing.

In this book, I'll share what I've learned over the years and the many mindshifts that occurred during that journey at Clermont Park. The experience completely challenged my own long-held beliefs and changed my thinking about what is possible in our communities. I'm not an expert on organizational change or a college professor. I'm just someone who has been working to transform the way we do things in senior living for many years and who has had the opportunity to learn from many, many people and situations.

My goal in writing this book is to share the mistakes I've made and the things I've learned over the last two decades working in this field. Along the way, I learned about the role that ageism plays in our communities and how our current focus on hospitality undermines many of the things that are important to well-being. I learned about the importance of purpose, growth, and inclusion, new approaches to driving organizational change, and the way that building design can promote a healthier community.

At the time this book published, I had begun to serve as the president and CEO of The Eden Alternative; however, the vast majority of this book was written from the vantage point of a senior living community operator and includes mostly stories from my time working in nursing homes, assisted living communities, and life plan or continuing care retirement communities. While the book is focused on my experiences in mostly market rate and upscale senior living settings, I think you'll find that many of the concepts and philosophies can be applied in a general sense to the way we view and support older people wherever they may live and are adaptable no matter how living environments continue to evolve over time.

I must also add a quick word about words. The words we use have an incredible impact on our thoughts and actions and on the cultures we create in our organizations. You'll notice that, unless I'm quoting someone directly, I use the term *community* instead of *facility* and that I use the terms *resident, older adult, older person*, and *elder* interchangeably. *Elder* is the preferred term used by The Eden Alternative and other culture change organizations, as it refers to someone who should be held in high esteem. I also refer to "senior living" in the title and throughout the book. I don't like that phrase, nor do I like the word *senior*, but as of today, no one has come up with a better term for "congregate living for older people." It's a balance finding words that the reader can relate to while honoring the language of person-directed care and support.

You'll find that this isn't necessarily a "how-to" book. It's a book about the mindshifts that must occur to create a different future. In the same way that AARP's Disrupt Aging focuses on changing the conversation about what it means to get older, this book focuses on changing the conversation about the way that we provide services and support for older people.

Transformation can begin at the moment we begin challenging our own thought processes. As community-building expert Peter Block says: "The shift in the world begins with a shift in our thinking. Shifting our thinking does not change the world, but it creates a condition where the shift in the world becomes possible."

The type of transformation we'll explore is adaptive work (more on that in chapter 9), which requires a lot of introspection and conversations with everyone in your community. At the end of each chapter you'll find "Questions for Discussion and Introspection" to help you start on that journey.

I hope this book will challenge and inspire you to push back against the status quo and drive deep and lasting change. You may find that you and your organization are already doing the things we'll talk about in this book. In that case, I hope you'll find it validating. Other things, I hope, will make you stop and think and perhaps spark some new ideas and conversations in your organization.

We've made progress, but we still have a long way to go.

When I was interviewing professionals in our field for this book, John Cochrane, president and CEO of HumanGood, shared his belief that we need a deep cultural shift to occur but we are so enmeshed in the status quo that we can't see ourselves as we really are. "Someone," he said, "will come along and disrupt our current framework and break through to a new way of thinking."

That someone should be us.

CHAPTER 1

Stranded

~~~~~~~~~~~~~~~~~~~~~~~~

A New Perspective on Senior Living

ONE OF THE BIGGEST conundrums that leaders in the field of senior living face is not knowing what it's like to be on the receiving end of the services and support we provide. This lack of perspective limits us and makes it far too easy to accept the status quo. A shift in perspective can help us to see things in a whole new way.

Twenty-Four Hours in a Nursing Home

I've always tried to see things from the vantage point of a resident. When I first became a nursing home administrator, I stayed as a resident for 24 hours, an experience I highly recommend to anyone working in our field.

My friends and colleagues thought I was crazy, but I wanted to understand what it felt like to be on the receiving end of our policies, systems, and processes. So I asked my team to come up with a typical diagnosis for someone coming in for a short-term rehabilitation stay and to admit and treat me like a resident. They were a little scared at first, but then they started having fun with the process.

They came up with a long list of problems and diagnoses for me. I was admitted as a woman in her 80s who had been living at home with dementia. Following a fall, according to their admission notes, I had surgery and treatment for a broken hip and arm. I was flagged as both a fall and wander risk and as needing significant support with incontinence.

After spending only 24 hours seeing things from a resident's vantage point, I was deeply disturbed. I realized just how much work

9

needed to be done in nursing homes. I've repeated this experience three more times at other very high-quality communities and have experienced many troubling things.

I've been rolled into my room and left to stare at the wall. I've been in rooms with roommates who were in the process of dying or who called out at night. I've lain in my narrow bed with its crinkly crackly mattress and uncomfortable pillow, dreading the next knock on the door that would come with alarming regularity throughout the night.

I've been woken up in the wee hours of the morning, and then left to sit lined up in the hallway with other residents, waiting for breakfast. I've been driven nearly mad by the incessant pinging and beeping of nurse call systems and bed alarms. I've had bed alarms and chair alarms placed on me and been restrained by a "lap buddy"—a misleadingly named cushion that is jammed into the front of a wheelchair to prevent you from rising. I've been seated at a "feeder table" reserved for those who need assistance with dining. I've felt lonely. And depressed. And helpless.

During each of these stays, I kept a video or written diary of my experiences. Below is a compilation of some diary entries from my different stays:

(*8:00 a.m.*) I have wheeled myself from breakfast and am sitting outside my room. I'm so tired, and other residents are sleeping in front of the TV. There's nothing to do. I'm angry! Why did they get us up so early just to have us sitting around doing nothing? I also have a profound feeling of sadness. Staff are standing at the nurses' station talking. Everyone is running around with their papers looking very busy while we are all just sitting here. I can't IMAGINE living this way. I suppose you adapt and give up after a while. I want to cry.

(*2:00 p.m.*) I'm sitting alone in my room doing nothing. I feel like going out and ripping the call light system off the wall. The beeping noises are incessant. And there are also all of the beeping noises of chair alarms. It's driving me crazy!!

(*5:30 p.m.*) There is a certain time of day when everything is unbearably sad. Most of the department directors have stopped in to say goodbye as they leave for the evening. I'm still sitting in my room in my wheelchair, where I was parked by staff, facing the window. I can see everyone walking through the parking lot to their cars in the fading light. They wave to me. I feel so sad. I never realized how it would feel to realize everyone is going home but you.

(11:00 p.m.) Woken by a knock on the door and staff putting clean towels in the room.

(12:00 a.m.) Woken again when staff came in and turned on the light to reposition my roommate.

(12:30 a.m.) Nurse and CNA came in to check my vitals per doctor orders.

(2:00 a.m.) Woken again when staff came in and flipped on the light to reposition my roommate.

(4:00 a.m.) I'm on edge waiting for the next knock on the door. It's startling. Now I can't sleep. I don't understand how people are supposed to function or be healthy with no sleep. I would definitely be an aggressive resident and hit people if this was my life and I was woken up all night every night.

(5:30 a.m.) Startled awake by a knock on the door. A nurse walked in and turned on the light. I covered my head with the blanket. She took my vitals and said she needed to check my skin for breakdown and other potential problems. "You've got to be kidding," I said. She wasn't.

(6:00 a.m.) Told it was time to get up for breakfast.

After each experience, I'd drag my sleep-deprived body out of the building, discharge papers in hand, squinting my eyes in the bright sunlight. Then I'd go home and cry. I'd end up in such a funk that it would take at least two full days to feel like myself again. And this was after living as a resident for only 24 hours and knowing it was a temporary situation. I can't imagine the devastating impact of living this way for months or years.

It's these experiments that have driven me to create change—it infuriated me that this was the way so many elders spent the last few years of their lives.

Before each experience, people would say that I'd never get a true picture of what life is like in a nursing home because the team members knew I was the boss and would be on their best behavior. But what I learned is that most of the awful experiences of living in a nursing home *aren't* due to people breaking the rules and doing their own thing;

it's people doing exactly what they're told to do! The problem is us—the formal leaders. It's our systems and rules and processes.

As impactful and important as these experiences were, there was an important element that was missing. In each of these situations, I was just playing a role. I was still completely in control. I knew I was going home the next day. I knew if things did get bad, I could jump out of bed and pull rank as the administrator. And I always knew I had the option to get up in the middle of the night, jump in my car, and hightail it home to a quiet bedroom with a comfortable bed. The opportunity to learn what it's like when you lose that control came years later—during a vacation gone wrong.

Stranded

It was fall 2014. My husband and I were packing for a much-anticipated vacation to Los Cabos, Mexico. As we stuffed our suitcases with shorts and bathing suits, we heard on the news that a hurricane was brewing off the coast in the Pacific Ocean.

Being a perpetual worrier, I wanted to cancel the trip. My husband, however, had other thoughts. "Cabo hasn't been hit by a hurricane in decades. We don't have anything to worry about," I remember him saying after he looked at historical storm activity in the area.

So we went. And it turns out that while my husband has a great many talents, weather forecasting isn't one of them. The day after we arrived, the storm strengthened, changed directions quickly, and was headed straight for us. We tried desperately to find a flight out, or even a bus that could take us outside of the projected area of impact, but had no luck. Unable to find an escape route, we were trapped in the direct path of Hurricane Odile, a category 4 storm and one of the most powerful hurricanes to ever hit the region.

As the dire nature of the situation became clear, the staff of the resort began urgent preparations for the storm. We watched warily as they scurried around the property, boarding up windows and moving pool furniture inside. That afternoon, we were rounded up, along with 300 other guests, and taken to the ballroom, the designated resort storm shelter, for the night.

The ballroom was packed with endless neat rows of chaise lounges, each with a towel, blanket, and pillow resting upon it. As we filed into the shelter, we were asked for our blood type and contact information for our next of kin. We were then assigned to a chair that would be our home for the duration of the storm. As we settled in for the evening, I remember laughing with the people in neighboring lounge chairs, certain that the next day we would again be relaxing by the pool, enjoying cocktails, and joking about our hurricane experience.

As the night wore on, our laughter stopped. We could hear the wind howling and objects hitting the building. Then the shrieking sounds started, the sound of metal being ripped apart above us. Ceiling tiles started falling. We ran, many of us crying and screaming, to the basement. There, we rode out the rest of the storm, huddled together at tables in the staff cafeteria and under racks of uniforms in the laundry room, every crash and every creak of the building sending new waves of fear through the group.

After the hurricane ended and we were allowed out of the basement the next morning, we saw how powerful the storm had been. Debris and glass were scattered throughout the property. The roof of our ballroom shelter was gone. The staff told us that the airport was destroyed, the roads were impassable, and there was no power or phone service anywhere in the region. And, because few people had made any preparations prior to the storm, looting and violence had already started in the area.

We ended up being trapped at the resort for 4 days until we could be evacuated.

I've given a lot of talks about this experience. While many people like to hear the details of the night of the hurricane itself, the real story, and the real opportunities for learning, came in the days after the storm. It was during that time, when we were trapped together at the resort, that we experienced the life that is led by so many elders in institutional settings. We experienced the regimented rules, the limited opportunities for purpose, and the overwhelming feelings of helplessness that plague so many older people.

The people who worked at that resort were much like those who work in the aging services field. They were dedicated, competent, and caring. Despite the fact that many of them had lost their own homes, they stayed with us and took care of us during the entire ordeal. Committed as they were, however, their demeanor changed when the storm hit.

"Vacation is over," they told us. "You are no longer guests. You are refugees who must obey our commands."

They emptied our mini bars and locked up every drop of alcohol in the resort, instructed us that we were to remain in our rooms or within a designated small safe area of the property at all times, and handed out information sheets detailing the rules we had to follow and scheduled times for meals.

They went from being the people who stood by eager and ready to grant us our every customer service wish to being the people who were in charge of our lives.

I understand why they took those steps. They were responsible for us and our safety. As we know from our own work in senior living, it's much easier and more efficient to care for people and keep them safe when there are stringent rules and systems in place. I've implemented and carried out such systems for years. These rules, unfortunately, often serve to institutionalize people.

As a student and teacher in the culture change movement, I thought I had a pretty good grasp of the mechanics and the impact of institutional practices. But, up until this point, I had only experienced institutionalization from the vantage point of the person who holds the power. Other than my short stints as a "resident," I'd never been on the receiving end. This shift in perspective was a big awakening for me. It helped me to understand what it must feel like to be an elder moving from a life of independence into a traditional senior living environment. There's an abrupt and deeply unsettling transition that occurs when you realize that you have to trade in your freedom, choices, and self-determination because you need someone to protect and take care of you.

It wasn't that we weren't cared for. Much like the staff of senior living communities, those resort team members took care of all our basic needs. They found enough relatively undamaged rooms throughout the resort for all of us to have a bed to sleep in while we waited to be rescued. They had adequate fuel in the generator to provide a couple of hours of electricity each day. They secured the property and kept looters from entering. They cooked for us and made sure we didn't go hungry.

While our basic needs were taken care of, we wanted more. And some very strange things started happening that, now, looking back, I realize are eerily similar to what we often see in institutional nursing homes, assisted living, and independent living settings. We experienced what many institutionalized older adults experience—what The Eden Alternative calls the three plagues of loneliness, helplessness, and boredom.

Loneliness

The deep feelings of loneliness that come from being trapped with strangers in an unfamiliar place set in immediately. While there were hundreds of people there at that resort with us, we were desperately lonely for home, for the familiar, and for our families. The cell towers were demolished, and we knew there was no cell phone service. But everywhere I looked, I saw people walking around carrying their cell phones and holding them up to the sky every few minutes, searching desperately for a signal. There were so many times that I heard people making statements that we hear so often in institutional settings: "I need to talk to my mother." "I need to talk to my sister." "Please, I need to find a way to talk to my kids."

This longing for home, and the familiar, was all consuming. Each day, the resort staff shared the latest updates with us, explaining that they were diligently working to find out when we would be able to go home. "We're trying to get you out of here," they'd say patiently. "As soon as we know something, you'll be the first to know."

We refused to accept that answer. We were desperate for information and some sort of validation that this experience would be ending soon. All day long, as we wandered aimlessly around the secured area of the property, we would watch for staff members to appear and would run up to them, pleading, much like a resident of a nursing home: "Please, I need to go home. When can I go home?"

Helplessness

We also experienced terrifying feelings of helplessness and powerlessness. In an effort to fight those feelings, I offered to help the staff. Soon after the storm had passed, I walked up to them and said, "Can I help you with something? I have years of experience in planning for disasters. Please, let me do something."

Expecting that my help would be welcomed, I was devastated when they instead just smiled, patted my hand, and said, "Thanks so much. That's great that you want to help. But we don't need your assistance. We've got this covered."

I think back now, to how many times I've responded in the exact same way to residents who have offered to help. How I thought I was easing their minds and their burdens by telling them I would take care of them.

I realize now how painful it is to be told that you have no role to play.

Other refugees had this same desperate need for purpose. Soon after we were released from the basement, I watched a group of men pick up shovels and start to clean up the branches, shards of clay roof tile, and pieces of glass that were scattered everywhere.

Within minutes, the resort general manager ran out and yelled, "Stop! You have to stop! It's not safe!" The refugees offered to sign a waiver and begged to continue their work so they would have some opportunity to make a difference. Again, the general manager refused. "Our risk management policy would never allow this," he said. "Only staff can do this work. We don't want you to get hurt." Defeated, the would-be volunteers went back to milling around, worrying, searching for cell phone signals, and watching the staff work.

This is the situation many elders find themselves living in: they are desperate for opportunities for real meaning and purpose, but we, as senior living providers, are so fearful of someone getting hurt or being sued or violating regulations that we strip away those opportunities. By doing so, we take away their right to make their own decisions about risk. It's clear to me now that the opportunity for control and purpose often outweigh any fear of being injured.

When it became clear that we had no purpose and no role to play, we became helpless.

Once, after sharing this experience at a conference, a woman from the audience approached me and said that her sister had been trapped in New Orleans during Hurricane Katrina. Her sister had no one taking care of her, the woman told me. She was left to fend for herself, but strangers banded together to help each other survive. She wondered why this hadn't happened with the people at my resort and hypothesized that because we were relegated to being helpless refugees, we quickly regressed and became dependent. With no opportunities for purpose, she surmised, we no longer felt a pull to improve the situation and instead became focused on ourselves and our own needs.

Her theory rings true to me. We became a bit like rebellious teens in some ways, fighting back against those who were trying to keep us safe. Intellectually, we knew that we were being confined to our rooms and to that small area of the resort for our own good. The hurricane damage, looting, and violence made the outside world dangerous.

That logic, however, didn't matter. We wanted to escape and explore the area.

We would wait until the staff members turned their backs, and then we would run away to the beach or the golf course. After our own escape attempt was squelched, my husband and I watched as other people ran off, only to be dragged back by the staff, time and time again. If resorts had wander management systems (devices that many nursing homes and assisted living communities use to prevent residents who are living with dementia from leaving), all of us would have been locked in.

I've been asked why we would try to escape when we knew it could be dangerous. I think one reason is that we had a very basic desire to want to see what was out there, beyond our boundaries. But more importantly, we ran away because no matter how dangerous things were, we didn't want to be told where we could and couldn't go and what we could and couldn't do. The drive for freedom, independence, and self-determination is an innate part of who we are as human beings.

That need doesn't change with age.

This experience completely shifted my thinking on secured memory support communities and the reasons behind what are often referred to as behaviors, wandering, and elopements. All these years I had thought of wander management systems as simply a means to keep people safe. I didn't understand how locked communities could become a prison to those who live there or how feeling trapped could trigger desperate and very human attempts to regain freedom and independence.

Boredom

After spending much of their time trying to herd us back to safety, the staff tried to distract us by bringing out some board games and decks of cards. Most people ignored the games, but one afternoon, I tried to play a game of cards with a small group. I was shocked to find that I lacked the focus and concentration needed to play a simple game of rummy. After a while, I gave up and wandered back to my room.

I understand now how elders may feel in our communities. I've sat in many meetings focused on residents who didn't want to participate in activity programs. We'd try, and fail, to figure out why they weren't interested. It makes sense to me now. It's inconceivable to think that we can take away the opportunity for purposeful work, and meaningful things to do, and try to replace these basic activities of real life with card games, bingo, and entertainment.

And, like elders living in an institution, mealtimes took on great importance for us. As most of us who work in the field know, it's not uncommon in senior living settings to see residents lined up outside the dining room an hour or so before meals start. We resort refugees did the same thing.

Lunch, for example, was scheduled at 1:00 p.m. every day. By 11:30 a.m., my husband and I would be sitting in our room, and one of us would say to the other, "We should probably head down there."

"Yep," the other would reply. "We might as well. At least there are other people there. Who knows, maybe something interesting will happen."

The other refugees had the same idea. Most of us were lined up outside the restaurant long before it was scheduled to open.

Prior to this experience, I never really dug down into the real reason that lining up for meals occurs in so many communities. I'm ashamed to admit it, but I think I believed that it had something to do with aging. That, as one senior living professional told me, older people have a "herd mentality"—or that when we get older we simply develop the need to eat and arrive at events earlier. I now understand that it has nothing to do with age and everything to do with sheer boredom and the lack of control that exists in many living environments.

Food Hoarding

When days are filled with nothingness, mealtimes become the main attraction. And food becomes a prized resource. Most of us who work in the field have known a resident who sits in the dining room and stuffs packets of sugar and crackers in her purse to hide in a drawer in her room.

I became that woman. I had found a plastic bag in my luggage and I brought it with me to every meal. When no one was looking, I stole crackers, and bread, and anything else I could get my hands on. And I brought the stolen goods back to our room and hid them. Within 24 hours of living in this situation, I became a food hoarder.

I was told once, long ago, that nursing home residents hoard food because they lived through the Great Depression. I believed that explanation for many years. But I never experienced any kind of scarcity in my life, and I certainly wasn't alive during the Great Depression. I stole food because I had lost all control over my environment.

I actually had voices inside my head that I believe are similar to the voices inside that woman's head in the nursing home. I heard one voice saying, "There's no food available other than at scheduled meal times. What if you get hungry at midnight?" And a scarier voice saying, "You have zero control in this situation. What if these people who you're counting on don't come through for you tomorrow?" Like the resident who smuggles crackers in her purse, my food hoarding had nothing to do with my social history or psychological well-being. I was simply responding to being in a situation in which I had no control.

Institutionalization

The basic truth of this experience is that, within a frighteningly short period of time, all of us who were trapped at that resort were institutionalized. And we were institutionalized by people who are very much like those who work in the aging services field—dedicated people who just wanted to take care of us and keep us safe.

It was amazing how differently we all responded to this experience. We met another guest, a woman who had also been stealing and hoarding food. One night she became so angry and upset that she started throwing food around her room, screaming at her boyfriend, and then ran out of the room in the middle of the night with staff chasing after her. She was a petite woman, but she was fighting so hard that it took two security guards to drag her back to her room.

Another guest was belligerent and angry, mainly concerned about the absence of alcohol. He yelled at the staff members constantly and walked around the resort, whispering and begging us to help him overthrow management and forcefully take control of the resort.

My husband dealt with the difficulty of the situation by sleeping. It was 90 degrees, with no air conditioning. This is a man who hates to be hot and normally can't doze off unless the temperature is below 70 degrees. Yet he slept constantly. The strong pull to escape a situation he didn't want to be in overrode everything.

I, on the other hand, couldn't sleep at all. I was agitated and couldn't sit still. I paced constantly.

I also started losing track of the days and losing track of time. One day, someone asked me what time it was. I looked at my watch and replied, "It's 9:30." There was no doubt in my mind that it was 9:30 in the morning and we had just had breakfast. I was shocked when my husband corrected me and told me it was actually 3:30 in the afternoon. I had become so confused that I was unable to read my watch or to realize that I had lost an entire part of a day. This, coupled with my inability to play a simple card game, illuminated what I now understand to be a marked decrease in my cognitive functioning.

The most disturbing epiphany of this whole experience was the realization that if we resort refugees were people in our 80s instead of our 40s, and were living in a typical nursing home or senior living community, we would be labeled as having "behaviors." We would be diagnosed with cognitive loss and a myriad of other problems. We would have care plans and medications prescribed to treat our symptoms.

Were we residents of an institutional senior living setting, I would have been diagnosed with an anxiety disorder, the early stages of dementia, and hoarding tendencies. My husband would have been deemed depressed. The woman who was throwing food and the man who was trying to overthrow management would be put on psychotropic medications.

Sometimes, when I'm giving a talk on this subject, I'll see people in the audience smile and laugh when I get to this point of my presentation. They understand how ridiculous it would be to label and diagnose and medicate people who were just exhibiting a normal human response to living in a difficult situation.

Then I see the expression on their faces change as they come to the uncomfortable realization that this is exactly what happens each and every day to thousands of older people in our country.

While the most drastic examples of institutionalization occur in nursing home settings, stringent rules, paternalism, and the stripping away of purpose and independence exist in all areas of senior living. Right this minute, there are countless older people who seem confused, not due to dementia, but to the mind-numbing effects of living in an institution. There are others who are reacting to their loss of power and purpose and freedom by "acting out," trying to escape, and self-isolating. And right this minute, medical professionals are writing care plans, prescriptions, and orders for psychological evaluations to address these conditions.

Despite our work toward person-directed care and services, we're still missing the basics. The problems we see with older people are often not due to aging, or to something being inherently "wrong" with the individual.

The problem is the situation that they're living in.

We resort refugees were institutionalized for a mere four days. How much worse would the confusion, depression, and anxiety have become if we had been trapped there for weeks, or years? It's a terrifying thought. Yet this is the life that many elders live.

We've made progress in designing more appealing living spaces and enhancing customer service. Many new communities look and function much like the beautiful "before" pictures of our upscale resort. But cosmetic changes don't fix the problem. Even in these beautiful settings, people can feel more like resort refugees than honored guests.

Experiencing life, even for a very short time, in an institution taught me that change won't come from new programs or surface-level initiatives. Changing the culture of senior living requires a thorough examination of our beliefs and practices, as well as a fundamental shift in the way we think about aging, our communities, and our roles as senior living providers.

Questions for Discussion and Introspection

Have you ever been in a situation where you experienced institutional practices? How did it make you feel? How did you respond?

What are your feelings about experiencing life as a resident in the community where you work? Why might you avoid such an experience?

In what way are there similarities between the "behaviors" of the resort refugees in this story and what you see happening with residents in your community?

How do you think you would respond to being in a situation where you were trapped and institutionalized? What "behaviors" might you have?

What situations are occurring in your community that are now thought of as "behaviors" that could be caused by the environment or systems currently in place?

CHAPTER 2

How May I Harm You?

The Pitfalls of the Hospitality Model

I'VE COME TO BELIEVE that the field of aging services has long lacked an identity of its own. The institutional nursing home examples that I shared in the Introduction and first chapter were spawned by our clinical, sterile hospital roots. We cared for older people under that institutional framework for a long time. Then we realized that this model wasn't a good fit. We *weren't* hospitals and *shouldn't* be hospitals. Hospitals, after all, are designed for short-term, acute health problems, not for long-term living.

We knew the aging baby boomers would demand something different, so we looked for something else to grab on to—something to model ourselves after—and we found the hospitality model. We began to adjust, building new hotel-like buildings, hiring hotel general managers, and adding resort-style training programs and amenities.

Coming from a master's program in hospitality, I believed for many years that this model was the answer and that senior living communities were, in essence, extended-stay hotels. However, I've discovered over time that the hospitality approach, in many ways, is just as poor of a fit for senior living as the hospital model was. Hotels and resorts are designed to provide an escape from real life. They're temporary fantasy environments where everything is done for you and you can sleep away the day, lounge by a pool, and eat gourmet meals—all without making your bed in the morning. But senior living isn't a respite from the real world, or a temporary fantasy life.

It *is* life. And that requires a very different approach.

Who Wants to Live in a Hotel?

As I shared in the Introduction, my mom lives with an incurable, progressive retinal disease. A few years ago, when the disease had started to significantly impact her life, my parents decided to move to a retirement community. As they investigated their options, they visited numerous places in different parts of the country. I accompanied them on some of the visits and was able to understand, for the first time, what these communities feel like from a consumer perspective.

One community tour stands out in my mind. It was a gorgeous building, clearly modeled after an upscale hotel. The lobby was beautiful. The interior design, artwork, services, and amenities were fantastic. As we walked through the building, I watched my parents' faces light up as we explored the large beautiful apartment homes, restaurants, and cocktail bar areas. I could picture them relaxing there, having fun with friends in the evenings. When we learned about the extensive concierge offerings and complimentary valet services, even I was ready to say "Sign me up!"

At one point in the tour, we paused as the sales counselor spoke with a resident. My folks looked at me, with wide eyes and big smiles, and whispered, "This place is amazing! It's just like a hotel!" They were thrilled.

Before making a final decision, they decided to go back for a visit, stay overnight in a guest room, and experience what life would be like as residents for a couple days.

I called them after their visit to see how it went. Rather than being excited, as I'd expected, they sounded down in the dumps. They told me they were considering completely scrapping their plans for moving into a community. They explained that the food was wonderful and the service was impeccable. "But," they said, "it's just like a hotel . . . except there are a bunch of old people."

They went on to explain that it just didn't feel like a community. Residents were polite to each other but didn't seem to be truly engaged. It seemed that everyone had well-established, and closed, social circles. Team members provided great customer service, but the relationships didn't feel authentic.

It seemed, they said, like the whole focus was on doing *for* the residents rather than promoting purpose and meaningful roles in the community. To make things worse, they had attended a resident council meeting where the executive director replied to most questions by saying he would have to ask the corporate office for approval on suggestions and requests. When my parents saw beyond the beautiful hotel-like appearance, they realized that this was a place that would likely leave them feeling dependent and lonely.

This was exactly the culture that they feared when they started considering moving to a community.

This is the danger of taking the philosophy, structure, and operating processes of a hotel or resort, sprinkling in some healthcare, and offering it up as a senior living community. We can wind up with beautiful buildings, stunning spaces, and spectacular services and amenities, but also with a culture that feels sterile, cold, and institutional, with few opportunities for engagement, purpose, or meaning. As environmental gerontologist Emi Kiyota so aptly concluded, "Elders living in grass huts in Africa with children at their feet are often happier than people in assisted living homes with a chandelier over their heads."

We Need to Belong

Like my parents, many of us, at first blush, think that living in a hotel or resort would be wonderful. What could be bad about being in a beautiful place where someone else does the cooking and cleaning and attends to your every need? But talk with anyone who travels a lot for work. They'll tell you that life in a hotel isn't all it's cracked up to be. Often, it's a lonely and empty existence.

When I was in graduate school, I did a mini-internship with Four Seasons, a hotel company renowned for its customer service and amenities. I lived in a beautiful Four Seasons hotel suite for two weeks. I experienced the grandeur, the exceptional customer service, and the fantastic amenities. But once I got past my initial sense of awe, I quickly became lonely.

At the end of my workday, I had no one to eat dinner with or just sit and talk with. I tired of walking the surrounding neighborhoods and eating alone every night. If it weren't for the bell staff taking pity on me and inviting me to join them on outings a couple of times, I would likely have wound up feeling despondent and depressed.

This wasn't the fault of Four Seasons, nor did it indicate any shortcoming in the hotel's approach to service. Hotels, and the hospitality model, are simply not designed to introduce guests to the person in the room next door, to encourage the development of friendships and meaningful relationships, or to help guests feel they are part of a community.

All of us, no matter what our age, have a basic need to belong and to be part of something. We're hardwired to be a part of a group. Millions of years ago, our ancestors shared resources and gathered at hearths to eat and to socialize. They worked together to hunt and to protect the group. Survival was predicated on being a part of a network or community.

That same need for inclusion exists today. Research shows that those who feel a sense of belonging and who are part of a social network live longer and healthier lives. Those who are socially isolated, lacking contact with others, suffer. An AARP study found that loneliness, especially as it relates to social isolation factors has dire consequences for people's health. Studies show that isolation and loneliness are as deadly as obesity and smoking.[1] Isolation is so dangerous and so prevalent that it is now being referred to as a public health epidemic.[2]

I used to think that moving to a retirement community would address the isolation and loneliness issues that so many people experience in their homes. But proximity to other people isn't enough. In some senior living environments, an elder may find him- or herself as lonely and cut off from others as I was in that fancy Four Seasons hotel. In one study, conducted at a life plan community (also known as a continuing care retirement community), researchers found that about one in four independent living residents were socially isolated.[3] Similarly, in three public housing senior communities, researchers found that 43 percent of residents were moderately lonely and 26 percent were severely lonely.[4]

When we focus our efforts on becoming like hotels or resorts, we disregard the need for inclusion and underestimate the complexity of the senior living ecosystem. As much as we like to celebrate the gifts that come with aging, there are some very real, and challenging, issues that arise and that can lead to isolation.

Many residents in senior communities are living with mobility challenges that make it hard to get out and about and be around other people. Injuries, arthritis, and other degenerative conditions can make it downright painful for people to make the long trek from their apartment to the dining room. And those with wheelchairs or walkers can have even more difficulty maneuvering to and within common area spaces. I've known many folks who, over time, have found it's just easier to stay home in their apartment.

There are also many who live with vision challenges. When my parents moved into their community, my mom was unable to see to find her way independently to the fitness center or the library to meet with her book club. Learning to function on her own required the engagement of an occupational therapist who could help her learn to maneuver independently. It took months. And it's still a challenge. For some people living with low vision, the complexities of navigating a building can become so overwhelming that they simply give up. When a woman with limited sight moved into one of my communities, her daughters came to me to talk about their concerns. She had become a recluse in her last community. It was too hard to find her way around the building. The culture was one where no one reached out to her to help, so she just stopped leaving her apartment.

Similarly, people with hearing loss may begin to disengage because they can't hear their tablemates at dinner or the speaker at an educational program. One day, I was visiting an assisted living community and noticed team members conversing with a resident via a microphone hooked to headphones worn by the resident. The executive director told me that the woman had moved from a secured memory support community. In her prior living environment, she spoke rarely and was believed, by her doctor and caregivers, to have advanced dementia. When she arrived at her new home, however, one of the team members discovered this was not the case at all. The problem was that the woman had profound hearing loss. She had simply given up on trying to engage with the world and retreated into herself.

Those who are beginning to experience cognitive challenges may also shy away from social engagements as it becomes more difficult to participate in conversations and programs. Their spouses also often experience social isolation. The stigma surrounding dementia is often so strong that the person living with cognitive challenges, and the person's spouse, start to self-isolate.

Even incontinence challenges can lead to isolation, as some residents, in trying to prevent an embarrassing incident, avoid participating in events located in areas without a bathroom nearby. I've known residents who would only come to gatherings if they could easily exit the room to get to a bathroom. When we redeveloped the Clermont Park campus, many residents were focused on the proximity of restrooms to the new common area spaces we were building.

Finally, as mentioned in the Introduction, there often exists an unchecked culture of ageism and ableism in senior living settings (see also chapters 3 and 4). Cliques and bullying occur with alarming frequency. In the American Seniors Housing Association's "Make Them 'Feel at Home'" report, researchers found that three-fourths of the communities they studied had one or more residents mention cliques or difficulty making friends as what detracted from their sense of feeling at home.[5]

All these challenges add up to a very complex social system, one that the hotel or resort philosophy of operations simply doesn't equip us to deal with. We'll talk more about addressing the complexity of senior living and building a sense of community in chapter 5.

"Doing For" Can Do Harm

Customer service, the hallmark of the hospitality model, also has potential negative implications in senior living settings. Throughout my career, customer service was one of my favorite parts of the hospitality approach. I love providing great customer service. And I love receiving great customer service. To me, there's nothing more relaxing than going to an upscale all-inclusive resort with exceptional service where the staff anticipates my every need. Many of us like this type of pampering once in a while. The problem comes when this reliance on others is constant and unending.

When we create such scenarios in senior living settings—where we are constantly "doing for" people—we can actually do harm. Customer service, no matter how excellent, can actually undermine and disempower those we are trying to support by focusing solely on "doing for" and "creating experiences for" people, rather than creating an environment where people are encouraged and supported in doing for themselves and creating their own experiences. We'll discuss, in chapter 5, why even thinking of residents as "customers" is something we should reconsider.

These service efforts have good intentions. We tend to believe that we should eliminate every hardship for residents of our communities. Doing too much for people, however, can take a toll on well-being.

In his book *The Blue Zones*, Dan Buettner shares lessons learned from studying the people who have lived the longest and healthiest lives in "successful aging" pockets around the world. One of the key lessons from his research is that, to live well and live long, older people should inconvenience themselves a bit.[6] By doing things like raking, sweeping, and shoveling, Buettner says, people can naturally integrate activity into their days.

Similarly, Roger Landry, M.D., president of Masterpiece Living, an organization focused on promoting successful aging practices, has concerns about communities that do everything for residents, such as carrying groceries from their cars. "We think we're helping," Landry says, "but often we are taking away those normal activities of daily life that maintain muscle strength and mobility."[7] Bill Thomas, M.D., cofounder of The Eden Alternative, agrees, explaining that the human body will retain only the strength that it needs to perform the work that it is called upon to do each day.[8] When we do more for people than they need us to do, we can create unnecessary helplessness and decline.

Our customer service approach may also undermine our own efforts to change the view of senior living in the marketplace. So many organizations promise, through their brochures and websites, a "carefree" and "worry-free" lifestyle where residents don't have to lift a finger. But one of the main fears of getting old is the potential loss of independence.[9] In a study conducted in the United Kingdom, researchers found that people feared losing their independence more than death![10] While some people certainly enjoy and benefit from having services provided, there are others who cling to the ability to do for themselves as proof of autonomy. By selling that vision of a worry-free lifestyle with images of older adults sitting back relaxing without a care in the world and reliant on others to meet their needs, are we unwittingly reinforcing the fear of losing independence?

Finally, this carefree resort sales approach is rooted in, and perpetuates, the negative societal view of aging and older people. Our society believes that older adults have little to offer to the world, viewing them as no longer productive and a drain on society. Our current advertising and messaging unfortunately reinforce that view by portraying older adults as being just recipients of services and care. "Rather than playing into these negative prescriptive stereotypes," says Landry, "we must recognize that older people are an untapped wealth of human capital and promote meaningful purpose and contribution in society."[11] We'll explore the power of purpose further in chapter 7.

Why Disney *Shouldn't* Run Our Communities

The hospitality model also impacts the way we relate to, and view, our team members. A number of years ago, I read the book, *If Disney Ran Your Hospital: 9½ Things You Would Do Differently*. At the time, the book was popular among senior living providers, and I, like many of my colleagues, was entranced with Disney's approach to customer service. I started a training program for my team members, teaching them to think like cast members. I asked them to remember that they were at work to play a specific role—just like Mickey or Donald or Goofy. I gave them customer service scripts and taught them elevator speeches to describe their work. I asked them to smile and implored them to leave their problems at home and practice being "on stage" when they were in front of residents.

I realize now that wasn't the best approach.

Reflecting back, I realize that I really *wanted* my community to be like Disney. I wanted it to be the happiest place on Earth. And sometimes our communities are just that—full of joy and cheer. But the reality is that our communities can also be full of sadness and grief. Residents experience extremely difficult personal life transitions and losses. Spouses, friends, and neighbors get sick. And people die. Unlike the shiny perfection of a theme park or resort, which serves as a *break* from reality, real life happens in our communities.

Real life is best met and supported through real, deep, and authentic relationships.

I now firmly believe that, rather than promoting training programs that teach customer service scripts and cast-member mentality, we must focus on creating environments where team members are encouraged to bring their true and authentic selves to work each day. Instead of spending time and resources on perfecting superficial responses, we should be helping our team members to hone deeper growth, such as emotional intelligence, listening skills, and self-care, to process, and respond to, difficult situations in a healthy manner.

In addition to providing more authentic interactions for residents and families, this approach can also improve the work experience of team members themselves. People who work in senior living settings are involved with what psychologists call emotional labor, which entails managing feelings and emotions to meet the requirements of a job. When I asked my team members to smile when dealing with difficult emotional situations and to put their true selves aside as they stepped on stage with residents, I was asking them to "surface act"—to pretend they were happy no matter what emotions they were feeling. Surface acting, which is often utilized in jobs such as waitressing and other service positions, has been shown to lead to stress, lower job satisfaction, and health issues.[12]

Hotels and resorts also have very clear and defined lines between guests and employees. In most hotels, team members are expressly prohibited from fraternizing with guests and from using hotel amenities. This makes sense in these settings where there are short-term interactions and no reason for deep and meaningful relationships to develop. But in our communities, relationships are key. Authentic interactions come only from people knowing each other well and deeply.

Some senior living organizations are starting to understand the importance of valuing team members, not just as service providers, but also as an essential part of the community. Rather than banning employee participation in dining and recreation venues or policing the relationships that exist between team members and residents, these organizations have realized that a truly engaged community requires removing the walls and barriers and blurring the lines between residents and team members.

In these communities, interaction is encouraged by designing dining spaces, fitness centers, and other amenities to be enjoyed by residents and team members alike. Team members are encouraged to bring their passions to work and to do things outside of their job descriptions.

In one of my communities, the central supply coordinator started a quilting club. In another, the maintenance director (who was also a certified trainer) helped residents to learn to use equipment in the fitness center. As an executive director, I often taught art classes. Not only is this helpful for residents, but team members are also able to bring all their gifts to work to share with the community. With a workforce that is undoubtedly motivated by making a difference, this is a great way to capitalize on what draws people to our field.

During the Clermont Park redevelopment, we decided to move in this direction, by encouraging team members to be a part of the life of the community. We wanted to change the perception that they were "the help" and instead focus on opportunities for real and meaningful engagement.

Prior to the change, team members were restricted from using resident spaces and had to eat and spend break time in the breakroom (which was windowless and devoid of character). When we decided to encourage them instead to dine in the restaurants, take breaks on the patio, and work out in the fitness center, a number of skeptics said it would never work. They believed that it would lead to chaos and resident dissatisfaction and that we'd need to create a list of rules to police this new culture.

As it turned out, the residents loved it, and only one simple rule was needed: Residents have priority. If there isn't room in the fitness center or restaurant, team members step aside. It worked beautifully. Many of us ate lunch every day with residents, laughing and talking and just "being." One of our maintenance team members told me how much he loved having lunch with residents. "They used to see me as just the guy who fixes things in their apartment," he said, "Now they know me as Ernie, a human being." We speak often about building intergenerational relationships. One of the best opportunities is right in front of our noses—if we encourage real relationships to develop between residents and team members.

These authentic relationships also built trust. Because I, and the rest of the team members, knew and were known as human beings by residents, it became much easier to bring up new ideas for change or to talk about tough topics like rate increases.

To further build this culture, we started holding community meetings, including team members and residents, so everyone was on the same page and working together. When people see themselves as part of the same community, focused on the same goals, the whole dynamic changes.

Sometimes when I introduce this concept of true and authentic relationships between residents and team members, people get nervous. "What if there are inappropriate relationships?" they ask. "What if a team member doesn't understand boundaries?" That's always a risk. But I've worked with well over a thousand employees in my career and have always been a proponent of breaking down the barriers and building relationships. I can think of only one that used relationship building as an opportunity to take advantage of residents. That's 0.1 percent of the people I have worked with. And she would have done it no matter what the policy or approach to interactions with residents. We have far more opportunity for good things to come from this approach than bad.

A Balanced Approach to Hospitality

Lest my hotel school alumni association disown me, I must say that I believe there *is* a role for hospitality in our organizations. It just shouldn't be the entire picture, and it must be applied in a balanced way (we'll talk more about the recommended focus on community building in chapter 5).

One of the most interesting uses of the hospitality model that I've encountered comes from Cancer Treatment Centers of America. CTCA is a great example of an organization that has a crystal-clear understanding of the needs of the patients it serves. It uses hospitality to welcome both patients and their caregivers and to help them feel comfortable and at home when visiting any of their five cancer specialty hospitals. Most importantly, the organization uses a hospitality approach to give power back to patients.

CTCA's chief growth officer, Peter Yesawich, Ph.D., says that the organization understands that a cancer diagnosis upends a person's life, causing unspeakable stress and fear. It's often the first time in a person's life when everything feels like it's out of control. Therefore, CTCA does everything it can to reduce the related stress and angst. Because

80 percent of CTCA patients come from several hundred miles away, the team focuses on relieving all unnecessary travel stress. They book airline tickets and pick the patient up at the airport. Upon arrival at the hospital, a greeter is waiting at the ready to give a warm welcome—and usually a hug. The lobby is designed to minimize anxiety. Instead of overhead paging, there is calming piano music. Rather than typical medical waiting room chairs, patients and their families find a large fireplace with comfortable chairs and sofas.

Yesawich says that this first 90 to 120 seconds after entering the lobby can alter patients' perception of what is to come with their treatment. A clinical, institutional focus communicates to patients that they are defined by their disease and that the power is in the hands of the clinicians. The CTCA lobby and warm welcome send a message of warmth and focus on whole-person wellness.

In their hospital rooms, patients can easily control the lighting, temperature, and blinds from their bed and can order meals through their TV. Guest accommodations for caregivers are provided either on site or in adjacent facilities owned by CTCA. In infusion centers, usually large sterile spaces, CTCA patients have heated recliner chairs placed in private cubicles with a view of a relaxing scene. Every aspect of the patient experience is carefully orchestrated to eliminate unnecessary stressors so patients can focus on getting well.

Like CTCA, senior living organizations can use hospitality to set the stage and do what hospitality is best at doing—welcoming strangers. Like patients going to a hospital, people coming to visit or move into a community can be nervous and frightened. Excellent customer service, making people feel welcome through concierge and reception services, and move-in protocols are critical in these situations. We have much to learn from hotels and resorts and restaurants in creating a welcoming and warm first impression.

We should also continue to explore fun and new ideas from the hospitality realm. Innovative outdoor living spaces, contemporary design features, and new food trends can all help to keep our communities fresh and fun.

It's critical that each community determine what the hospitality model should look like and how it should function. This means involving residents, families, and team members and discussing the good and the bad and the ups and the downs of a customer service and hospitality approach. Where can hospitality be used effectively? Where could it be doing harm?

The approach must also be individualized. Residents who have a car, who volunteer outside the community, who have meaning and purpose and strong relationships may do just fine with a strong customer service approach. However, as people begin to develop challenges and those organic opportunities evaporate, we must adapt and leverage new opportunities to support independence.

One day, I visited an assisted living memory support small home. The building featured an open kitchen and living area that were designed for resident engagement. However, using the space as it was designed took a lot of focus. When a resident wants a glass of juice, for example, team members should help the resident to get a glass and pour the juice herself rather than jumping up and getting it for her. "We have to un-train our new team members on what they've learned about hospitality at other communities," the team explained.

I'm often asked what a community should do if it wants to foster more independence, but some residents still want someone to carry their groceries or to have staff accompany them on outings. I think it comes down to this: Even if we know that a resident could maintain more physical function and autonomy by doing for herself, if she chooses not to, that's her decision. And it may be that doing some things for particular residents enables them to retain independence in other aspects of their lives. We must remove paternalism from the equation and support all residents in making their own well-informed decisions—whether we agree with them or not.

The most important thing to remember if considering adapting your organization's approach to service and hospitality is that modifications shouldn't be forced on a community or a resident. This type of change requires education and two-way dialogue.

~~~~~~~~~~

Questions for Discussion and Introspection

How prevalent is the hospitality and customer service approach in your community and organization? What are the positive and negative impacts of your current approach to hospitality and customer service?

Where do you see isolation occurring in your organization?

Review your website and marketing materials. What message are they sending about the role of older adults? Do they support or challenge the current negative views of aging? Are they brand focused and focused on what "we can do for you," or are they focused on the possibilities, purpose, and value of older adults?

Where could customer service be undermining opportunities for purpose?

What role do team members play in your organization? Are there opportunities to "blur the lines" between team members and residents?

How often are formal leaders engaged with residents in an informal manner, such as having lunch or just "being"?

CHAPTER 3

Who Wants to Get Old?

As WE DISCUSSED in the previous chapter, the use of the hospitality model is both rooted in and perpetuates the negative and inaccurate views of aging. Creating healthy cultures starts with understanding and addressing ageism.

We're All Aging

Right now, as you read this sentence, you're aging. We all are—every minute of every day. In youth, the passing of a day, a month, or a year isn't viewed as a negative because the passing of time means we're growing up. And growing up is viewed as a good thing. Many times, we'll hear kids describe their age as "7 and a half" or "almost 8" in anticipation of being one year older, and younger people excitedly look forward to the milestones in their future—being old enough to drive, graduating from college, landing a first job, getting a promotion, raising kids.

But then, as we move through our lives, "growing up" becomes "growing old," and it's no longer viewed as a positive thing. Many of us begin to downplay, or even fib about, our age. We mourn each passing year. Or we get so caught up in day-to-day life that we ignore the passing of time, and before we know it, decades have slipped by.

I was 27 when I became a nursing home administrator. Most of the people who reported to me were many years older than I. People would often comment on how young I was, and would ask questions like, "What's a young girl like you doing with a big job like this?"

Somewhere along the line, people stopped asking me that question. Without even realizing it, I had aged into my job. I never really gave much thought to getting older. Like many people, I had pushed the reality of aging and mortality from my mind as concepts that would be better considered much later in life.

That all changed in my mid-40s. After decades of pushing aside the realities of aging, I found myself ruminating about the finite truth of our existence… and about getting older. I thought about all the things that were unfinished in my life, and I started worrying about death and dying, particularly because I have no children and no one to take care of me in my old age. After months of sleepless nights worrying about these issues, I went to see a counselor and explained what I was feeling.

"Here's the thing," said my counselor, "I think you're in a midlife crisis."

I was shocked. I went home that night, burst through the door, muttering obscenities under my breath, and exclaimed to my husband, "Can you believe it? My counselor said I'm having a midlife crisis! How is that even possible?"

"Well," my husband said, tentatively, "the average life span for a woman is around 86. You're 46. So, actually, your midlife crisis should have happened three years ago. You're late."

At first I was indignant. And then I realized he was right. It was like a punch in the gut—this awareness that I had come to, and actually passed by, the midpoint of my life without even realizing it. For as long as I had worked with elders, it shouldn't have come as a surprise. I think, though, like many people, that I spent the first half of my life somehow pretending that getting old wouldn't happen to me.

But now, it was undeniable.

I had reached that uncomfortable awakening that most of us experience, if we live long enough. The realization that the stars of popular culture are young enough to be your children. The shock that comes from hearing about high school classmates dying from heart attacks or cancer. The understanding that the unhealthy choices of your youth eventually catch up with you. And the awareness that your own parents are now considered "elderly." It's at that midpoint in life that things can start to get extremely uncomfortable.

At the time of my epiphany, I had been studying ageism for a number of years as part of my work. But until that point, I'd been examining it only from the periphery. I believed that ageism was prejudice owned by other people, not by me. I couldn't be ageist—I work in senior living, for God's sake!

I thought because I had a very healthy level of respect and admiration for older people that I didn't harbor fear or negativity about the aging process. Looking back now, I think I believed that the residents in my retirement community were somehow different from me, that being old was a static state of being, instead of a phase of life that all of us, if we live long enough, will enter.

My counselor helped me to understand that this new perspective and period of time should be considered more of an awakening than a crisis, and that if I accepted it as such and took time to explore my beliefs and fears about aging, I could be not only a happier person but also a better leader. After all, how can one be an advocate for elders and an innovative thinker in the senior living field when harboring unresolved fears and issues about aging?

I suspect this is an issue that many of us need to grapple with.

Getting Old in America

It makes sense that we would avoid thinking about old age. We know that, unless things shift drastically in our society, getting old means we'll likely be looked down upon, pushed aside, pitied, and perhaps even laughed at. That's certainly not something to look forward to. So instead of facing reality, we spend exorbitant amounts of money, time, and energy in a desperate, and always unsuccessful, attempt to hold on to youth.

When we do honor aging, it's generally in the form of celebration of older folks who don't act their age and are able to keep up with the youngsters. We call them "rock stars" and "super agers," implying that the majority of older people, who *aren't* running marathons or climbing mountains, are somehow deficient. Beneath these pseudocelebrations of age, at the core is the message that value lies only in youthfulness. As my 20-something trainer at the gym once said to me, "It's not bad to be old as long as you seem like you're young."

As I've become more aware of ageism, I see it everywhere. Even at the grocery store. In my local store, a sign is posted in every checkout line that reads, "If you're lucky enough to look under 30, please have your ID ready." Even grocery stores are judging us on our age and appearance! I contacted the store and asked them to reconsider the wording on the sign. They were bewildered that anyone could find the sign offensive, even though the message was insulting the appearance of their typical grocery store patrons. The signs are still there.

We should be as shocked and mortified by a sign like this as we would be by a sign insulting people because of their race or gender. This type of message devalues a whole group of people and, as we'll see later in this chapter, has devastating consequences. But ageism is so commonplace that we seldom notice it, let alone question it.

The negative messaging is everywhere. Before even reaching that sign in the checkout lane, a walk through a typical grocery store bombards us with messages about our youth-obsessed culture. From the greeting card aisle stocked with cards showing mock sympathy at the advent of another birthday, to the hair coloring and antiaging wrinkle creams in the cosmetics aisles, we are told, clearly and without apology, that being old is something to be avoided at all cost.

Ageism is at the root of many of the challenges we face in senior living. Take, for example, the reticence of so many people to move into a retirement community. The commonly heard statements, "I'm not ready yet" or "I don't want to live with a bunch of old people," illustrate that, for many, a decision to make a move to a senior living community is a sign of giving up and accepting that one is, God forbid, old. This belief system is also at the root of much of the bullying, marginalization, and segregation of frail elders that occurs in senior living settings.

Our society's ageist beliefs also impact our ability to attract and retain team members. Tracey Gendron and her colleagues from Virginia Commonwealth University studied the career commitment of 756 people who work in the field of aging services. Their research found that aging anxiety (fear of one's own aging) had a negative relationship to career commitment, job satisfaction, and career motivation.[1] "The bottom line," says Gendron, "is that we have a recruiting and retention problem with ageism at the core."

Our field is currently focused on recruiting younger people to work in aging services. Rarely, however, do we dig into ageist beliefs that may be impacting our progress in attracting them. Like people at every age, the younger generation is impacted by the negative messaging about growing older. My former assistant, who was in her mid-20s, was one of those young people who "got it." She loved working with elders. But she often told me how odd it was to have conversations with her friends who were in "exciting" fields like medicine or law or finance. "They can't understand why I work here," she said. "It's like they think aging is a disease you can catch."

Indeed, a 2013 study examined 84 Facebook groups focused on older individuals. All of the groups' creators were under the age of 60, with many being in the 20 to 29 age group. Facebook's Community Standards, the researchers noted, state that hate speech is not tolerated and that singling out individuals based on religion, sex, gender, sexual orientation, disability, or disease constitutes a violation of the site's terms. Age was not listed, which led researchers to believe that many of the groups would focus on negative stereotypes of aging.

They were right. While there are now many Facebook groups focusing on positive aspects of aging, in this study researchers found that all but one of the group descriptions studied reflected very negative views of older people. One group description stated: "Old people are a pain in the [expletive deleted by study authors] as far as I'm concerned and they are a burden on society. I hate everything about them, from their hair nets in the rain to their white Velcro sneakers. They are cheap, they smell like [expletive deleted by study authors] . . . they are senile, they complain about everything, they couldn't hear a dump truck." Others suggested that elders should be banned from public activities such as shopping, face a firing squad, or participate in a voluntary euthanasia program.[2]

Imagine, instead, a society in which gray hair was a symbol of achievement and status rather than one of decline and helplessness. Perhaps rather than pretending that old age only happens to others, people would acknowledge earlier in life the facts of aging, make better lifestyle decisions, and put in place adequate financial plans for their futures. Perhaps elders would see the value that can come from living in a community setting and wouldn't feel the need to cling to their homes when their plan to age in place is no longer working for them. Maybe people would flock to careers in our field.

Covert Ageism

Ageist beliefs don't always show themselves in blatant discriminatory remarks. Often, they come under the guise of well-meaning compliments. We go to happy hour after work with our colleagues and happily exclaim "Thank you!" to the bartender who asks for identification to buy a drink. We praise and compliment people who look younger than they are and say things like, "You look great for your age!" and "60 is the new 50."

Even in the field of senior living services, we often hear people apologize for or hide their age. At a conference, we may hear a speaker from a senior living organization say, "I've been working in this field for 30 years. Of course, I started my first job when I was 12." On the bulletin boards of several professionals in the field of aging services, I've seen a cartoon that depicts an old woman sitting in a wheelchair looking at a shadow of herself on the wall as a young ballerina. "How others see you is not important. How you see yourself means everything," the caption reads. Even this seemingly positive cartoon has an underlying message that our value is rooted in our younger selves, not in who we are in elderhood.

Stereotyping is another often unrecognized component of ageism. When I'm interviewing job candidates, I'll often ask them why they want to work in a senior living community. "I love older folks!" many will say, "They have so much wisdom and are so nice." This, as with most types of prejudice, is an example of stereotyping. Researchers in the field of gerontology have pointed out the prevalence of generalizations about older people. But according to Ashton Applewhite, author of *This Chair Rocks: A Manifesto Against Ageism*, the longer we live, the more different from each other we actually become.[3]

As someone who has worked with elders for two decades, I can say without a doubt that not all old people are nice. And not all old people are wise. At any stage of life, some people are wise and kind, and some are not. When we stereotype, even in a seemingly positive way, we stop seeing people as individuals and pave the way for prejudice to take hold.

Paternalism

We must also become aware of paternalism, or acting for the good of another person without their will or consent, as it is often a symptom of ageist beliefs.

When my parents decided to relocate to my city and move into an apartment in a nearby retirement community, I was so relieved. I really didn't have to do much for the move. They were extremely independent and had handled all of the downsizing and the sale of their house, and they had hired a company to help them unpack and settle into their new home.

Their move should have been a breeze for me. But I was a wreck. A few days after they moved in, I called my parents from my office to see how they were doing. They mentioned they were having some struggles with getting their wireless Internet hooked up and that they were a little frustrated with things being disorganized and unsettled in their apartment, something that was extremely challenging for my mom with her vision loss. They were also trying to find a new doctor so my mom could get in for an appointment. They sounded tired and discouraged.

My parents told me they were fine and had things under control, but I panicked. I jumped up from my desk, got in my car, and sped over to the community. I hurried in and started going through boxes in their apartment and calling doctor offices. As I was rushing through the community to visit the concierge desk about the Internet issues, I ran into Patrick, a community team member who I had known for some time.

"How are you?" he asked.

"Not good!" I exclaimed, and began rambling through my list of worries, my eyes filling with tears.

Patrick stopped me. He put his hand on my shoulder and said, "Jill, have you ever heard of a helicopter parent?"

"Of course," I replied.

"Well, there's also something called a helicopter daughter," he said, "and you're being one. Your parents are fine. They're very competent. They'll get this all figured out. Let them handle things."

At first, I have to admit, I was a little peeved at him. Who was *he* to say what help my parents did and didn't need?

But he was right.

Here I was, a person with years of experience in supporting elders, and I had become *that* daughter. The one who thinks every problem is hers to solve. The one who thinks that just because her parents moved into a retirement community, they were suddenly helpless. The one who swoops in and tries to fix everything.

My behavior came from a place of love, but it also came from a place of ageist beliefs. The things my parents were going through were the normal stressors that anyone, no matter what their age, would experience after uprooting their lives and moving halfway across the country. They were more than capable of making decisions and handling things on their own. But because they're older, I thought I needed to fix everything for them.

Paternalistic thinking is all too common in senior living settings and most often results from how we think about aging and older people. (We'll spend more time exploring paternalism and how it impacts our risk management and decision making in chapter 8.)

The Intersection of Ageism and Ableism

Ableism is a close cousin to ageism. Defined as prejudice against people living with different physical or cognitive abilities, ableism often rears its ugly head when older people begin to experience challenges with mobility or cognition. Because our society places such value on independence, self-reliance, and youth, older people will often refuse devices or assistance, such as caregiver services, hearing aids, canes, and walkers. Even in senior living settings, this occurs frequently. People who do use assistive devices may be ostracized, marginalized, or bullied. This is such a significant challenge that I've devoted chapter 4 entirely to this topic.

One of the most striking intersections of ageism and ableism is the way in which we think about and talk about dementia. Take, for example, one of the most popular unfilmed screenplays of 2015. It was a comedy about former president Ronald Reagan and his life with Alzheimer's disease. Billed as a "hilarious political satire," the screenplay featured an intern tasked with convincing Reagan (originally to be played by Will Ferrell) that he is an actor playing the president in a movie.[4]

The Reagan family and the Alzheimer's Association were outraged. Ferrell wisely backed out and, to date, the movie has not been made. But this scenario begs the question: Why did Hollywood executives and numerous others think a comedy about Alzheimer's disease was appropriate? We would never see a comedy ridiculing someone living with Lou Gehrig's disease or autism, for example.

The answer likely lies in our negative views of aging and the way in which our society devalues older adults. Because Alzheimer's typically accompanies aging, we devalue those living with the disease. We joke about them. We marginalize them. And we segregate them from society.

For a moment, let's imagine a very different scenario, one in which the millions of people living with Alzheimer' disease and other types of dementia weren't old folks, but instead were kids. What would be different? Would we make a Hollywood comedy about these kids? Would we segregate them from their peers? And keep them in locked units? Or would we find ways to value and honor these children and keep them connected with people and society?

It's likely that we would see inclusive schools and playgrounds where kids living with dementia would be playing with their friends. Where their peers would be educated about dementia and would learn how to be a kind and supportive friend. And if there was even a whisper about a movie that would denigrate these kids or a mention of plans to segregate them, there would be boycotts and rallies and outraged celebrities fighting for change.

Alas, in day-to-day life, old people living with dementia don't generate this kind of passion from the general public. Ageist beliefs are far too ingrained and accepted in our society. Folks like dementia expert G. Allen Power, M.D., are challenging us to rethink segregation and secured neighborhoods, but the topic is still far from the mainstream. Changing our views of, and approach to, supporting people living with dementia requires changing our views of aging.

Societal Views of Aging

To comprehend, and begin to address, our societal views on aging, it helps to understand the way elders have been viewed throughout history. According to Jared Diamond, professor of geography and physiology at UCLA, there have always been cultures, and pockets of time, in which elders were disregarded, or even discarded. This occurred mainly within nomadic societies, where elders were unable to survive long journeys, and during times of scarce resources, such as famines.[5]

For the most part, however, elders have been revered throughout history. In his article, "Ageism: Prejudice Against Our Feared Future Self," Todd D. Nelson explains that in many societies, elders were the keepers of the culture and history of their people.[6] During biblical times, elders were so esteemed that if a person lived past the age of 50, he or she was considered to have been chosen by God for a divine purpose.[7]

Today, says Nelson, older people are treated as "second-class citizens with nothing to offer society."[8]

I remember a resident at one of my communities describing, with great frustration, the way she feels when she goes out into the world. "I feel like a doddering old fool out there," she told me one day, pointing to the window in my office. "I can't explain to you how awful it is to feel irrelevant."

Unfortunately, her experience is all too common. Researchers have found that the majority of people over the age of 60 have experienced ageism in the form of jokes poking fun at old age, not being taken seriously, and being ignored by others.[9]

According to Nelson, the role of older adults changed as a result of two broader changes in society. First, he attributes the invention of the printing press and its ability to mass produce and disseminate of information for stripping elders of their role as the resource for history and information.[10] Our reliance today on information gathering from the Internet further diminishes the traditional role of elders as a source of knowledge. I used to call my mom for everything, from recipes to advice on health symptoms. Now I find that information on the Internet. It's much easier to Google a topic than it is to find an older person to answer your question.

Nelson goes on to say that the Industrial Revolution also damaged the status of older people.[11] While our society once placed a high value on experience, the Industrial Revolution shifted to a focus on efficiency and the ability to adapt and learn new things quickly. In addition, this change required that families become highly mobile to relocate to where jobs were available. The extended family model, with multiple generations living under one roof, was less able to move and adapt to this new reality.

Further, as Diamond explains, America has developed a strong "cult of youth."[12] We celebrate independence and self-reliance. As some of these traits are lost through the aging process, the value of elders is diminished. This obsession with independence is a faulty notion, however, according to thought leaders like Bill Thomas, M.D., co-founder of The Eden Alternative. Thomas explains that none of us is truly independent at any time in our lives, and we should be striving for a healthy level of interdependence instead.[13] Regardless, most of us balk at acknowledging that we may need help. And those who need assistance are often seen as broken versions of their former selves.

Finally, because more people now live to old age, it's likely that we view this occurrence as less of an accomplishment.

Regardless of the reasons, negative messages about aging are everywhere. Exceptions exist, such as AARP's Movies for Grownups, which celebrates standout films with unique appeal to movie lovers with a grownup state of mind and recognizes the inspiring artists who make them. Far more often, however, movies, news stories, and TV shows depict elders as foolish, cranky, or pathetic. Skincare product advertisements urge us to combat wrinkles and fight aging, reminding mainly women that much of their value is based on retaining a youthful appearance.

The negative messaging works. As a nation, we spend billions of dollars on antiaging treatments. In 2012, pharmacy benefit management service Express Scripts reported that Americans with private insurance spent more on prescriptions to fight aging-related conditions such as mental alertness, sexual dysfunction, menopause, aging skin, and hair loss than they did on medications to treat diseases.[14]

The aging of the baby boomer generation has pushed our negative views about old age straight to the forefront. As the nation prepared for the phenomenon of a large cohort of old people, we began hearing warnings. A 2009 Forbes column predicted a future in which baby boomers would "begin migrating from factory floors and corner offices to wheelchairs and adult diapers."[15] Today, the aging boomer population is often referred to as a "silver tsunami," sending the message that the aging of society should be viewed as a disaster—one in which a large part of the population is no longer contributing and has become useless, debilitated, and a drain on resources.

These messages, surrounding us in everyday life, seep into our subconscious minds. As Kirsten Jacobs, Director of Dementia and Wellness Education at LeadingAge says, "It's in the air we breathe."[16] It's impossible that those working in the aging services field aren't impacted by these views, and that this negativity about aging doesn't influence the way we design buildings, the way we develop programs and services, and the way we make decisions within our communities.

How can we create environments that honor elders when we're harboring our own issues and prejudices about aging? To truly transform senior living, we must become acutely aware of the ageism that surrounds us and exists in our own minds—and become aggressive in our battle against it.

The Impact of Ageism

Unlike other types of prejudice, we will all be victims of ageism, assuming we live long enough. And these pessimistic views of old age cause significant damage. Research shows that if we believe the negative stereotypes about aging—that it's all downhill, that we become a drain on society, that we have no value—these beliefs become a self-fulfilling prophecy. For example, people with negative self-perceptions of aging are more likely to develop dementia and less likely to recover from a debilitating accident.[17]

The images and beliefs we hold also have an incredible impact on the way we function in day-to-day life. Researchers have found that those who are exposed to negative stereotypes about aging performed more poorly in the areas of memory, writing, and mathematics than those exposed to positive stereotypes.[18]

Even physical abilities are impacted by a person's mindset. In her paper, "Mind Matters: Cognitive and Physical Effects of Aging Self-Stereotypes," Becca R. Levy, Ph.D., of Yale University describes a study in which the gait speed and swing time (amount of time that the foot is lifted off the ground when walking) of older adults were measured before and after being exposed to aging stereotypes. Those who were exposed to positive aging stereotypes had significant increase in both swing time (indicating better balance) and gait speed. Incredibly, these improvements were similar to those experienced by older people who exercised rigorously for several weeks.[19]

What we believe about aging can also impact how long we live. Those who hold negative self-perceptions of aging are likely to die a whopping 7.5 years earlier than those who have positive views.[20]

When we change our beliefs, we change our lives.

The field of aging services has done much to develop success-ful aging initiatives and wellness and fitness programs. But few of us understand or put forth the resources needed to understand and counteract ageism, which clearly impacts well-being and health.

Similarly, our country has invested a significant amount of resources into reducing healthcare costs via traditional medical inter-ventions. What would happen if we also focused on changing society's views on aging? The evidence clearly indicates that people would live longer and healthier lives with, presumably, less need for costly medical interventions. In 2018, researchers at the Yale School of Public Health published a study detailing the intersection of ageism and healthcare expenditures. They estimate that ageism increases healthcare expendi-tures in the United States by a whopping $63 billion each year.[21]

It Starts with Us

If we want to transform our communities, strengthen our society, and change the perception of aging, we have to start with ourselves and work from the inside out. As Growing Bolder CEO Marc Middleton says, if we wait for institutional change to shift views of aging, it will be too late for all of us.[22] It will happen, he suggests, one person at a time. As AARP's Disrupt Aging initiative explains, changing our ageist culture requires that we examine and question our own deep-seated beliefs and fears about aging. And that's not an easy task. In the words of writer Sally Kempton, "It's hard to fight an enemy who has outposts in your head."

Because ageism is so prevalent and unquestioned in our daily lives, identifying it can be difficult. Becoming aware of the messages we're receiving requires intention and focus.

I often encourage groups I'm working with to commit to an ageism awareness challenge. The challenge requires that they set their intention on becoming hyperaware of negative messages about aging for a week. I ask them to pay attention to what they see when they're watching television and reading magazines, what they hear when they're at happy hour or chatting in the break room, and, most importantly, what they themselves are thinking and saying. I ask them to take notes of their experiences and to come back together and discuss their findings with the group. It's always eye-opening. For aging services providers, such an exercise can uncover the shocking extent to which negative views on aging impact our policies, our practices, and our organizations. As one person told me, "Once you learn about ageism and pay attention to it, you realize it is absolutely everywhere. Now I can't stop seeing it!"

Changing the Conversation

Once we become aware of the overt and covert examples of ageism and ableism around us, we must start to push back, change the conversation, and find ways to replace the negative stereotypes and messages with positive ones. For example, one simple step we can take is refusing to purchase birthday cards with negative aging messages. There are many other opportunities to shift people's thinking as well.

One day, I was talking with a group of women at a community. It was a casual conversation. They were talking about what a drag it is to get old—the wrinkles, the aches, the myriad doctor appointments, and so on. These ladies were lobbing ailments and complaints back and forth so quickly I could barely keep up.

It struck me that this was an opportunity to change the conversation. So, I asked this simple question: "What's awesome about aging?"

They looked at me like I was crazy.

"What kind of question is that?" One woman demanded, "Did you just ask us what's awesome about aging? You have to be joking."

"No." I said, "I mean it. Tell me what gets better as you get older?"

There was silence.

Finally, one woman said tentatively, "Well, you get discounts at stores."

They all nodded.

Another chimed in, "I have more free time now."

And then the conversation transitioned to a deeper level. The women began talking about the perspective and wisdom that come with age and the way in which they now understand what matters in life.

We started talking about the "happiness curve" and how numerous studies have found that people generally report higher levels of well-being in their later years than in middle age. We talked about the research suggesting that elders tend to better understand different points of view, and can more easily identify compromises and come up with more solutions to a problem than their younger counterparts.

This was all new information to them. At the end of the conversation, the women were noticeably happier, their voices full of excitement instead of dread. They sat up straighter and had a little more pep in their step when they left the room. These small interactions, when repeated over time, can shift the culture of aging in our communities.

I had a similar conversation with a colleague in the field who said that she was asked her favorite thing about aging. "I can't think of a thing!" she complained. "What's good about getting old? I have wrinkles! And everything is sagging!" As we talked, she was eventually able to identify some positive things about growing older. She said she has more money and resources than she did when she was younger. That her career and family life are much more fulfilling. That she's more confident and understands what's important in life.

Like the group of women, my colleague eventually got to a place where she could see the good things that come with age. But it took a 10-minute conversation to get to a point where she could verbalize concrete benefits of growing older.

If we, the people who work in this field, don't feel good about aging, how can we expect anyone else to?

We must work on constantly changing the status quo of aging to help ourselves, and others, begin to think differently. We can take inspiration from outspoken leaders such as Jo Ann Jenkins, AARP CEO and author of *Disrupt Aging: A Bold New Path to Living Your Best Life at Every Age*, who strive to raise awareness of aging stereotypes and help young and old alike to see the potential that older age presents to individuals and to society.

The opportunities are everywhere.

One morning, I was at my gym and was talking with my trainer about age. When I told her I was in my late 40s, she said, "Wow! You don't look that old. You look great!" I almost said what I would normally say, "Wow, thank you so much! You're my favorite person in the whole world." But I stopped myself, and instead said, "I know you're trying to be nice, but what would be wrong with looking like I'm in my late 40s?" She was taken aback by my response and didn't say much at the time. But she came back later and said she'd been thinking about that question a lot and had been reconsidering her views on getting old.

Sister Imelda Maurer, director and founder of In Service to Our Own, shared with me a fantastic story about a response she gave to an ageist comment. Sister Imelda Maurer had recently turned 80 and was at a hotel for a conference. She asked an employee for directions to a conference room. The man took her to a bank of elevators, and when the door opened, he gestured and said, "This way, young lady." Sensing that he was a friendly and well-meaning person unaware of the ageist bias in calling her a young lady, Sister Imelda turned to him and said, kindly, "When a person has achieved the age of 80, it is an accomplishment, and many of us do not want it disregarded." The man reflected for a moment and responded with a smile, "Oh, congratulations!"

By then, everyone in the elevator was smiling. "Thank you." Sister Imelda replied, "I like that a lot better."

It's these small interactions that can cause ripple effects in our society.

There is also much we can do to begin to inoculate future adults against ageism. Through cartoons and films, children are exposed to the same negative messaging about aging adults. Ageist stereotypes are even unwittingly promoted in some schools. It's become a trend, for example, to celebrate the 100th day of school by dressing like a 100-year-old. Pinterest and other websites provide instructions for parents to help their kids look and act the part, including avoiding any bold or bright colors and instead dressing in drab solid colors and using a "simple walking cane" to "hobble around with."[23] Another website recommends that parents encourage their child to call other people "Sonny" and "go a little overboard as a stereotypical old person to make it more fun."[24]

One parent described her son's perfectly put-together costume:

Kyle's wrinkles were the coolest and honestly they made him look utterly EXHAUSTED! He really looked his age. We kept asking him if he was tired and Kenzie thought he was making dirty faces at her since the wrinkles kind of gave him a permanent scowl. Too funny![25]

When Kelly Papa, Corporate Director of Learning at Masonicare, learned that her child's school was holding one of these "dress like a 100-year-old" days, she was horrified. Papa admits she had some hesitation in contacting the teacher, but she realized she had to take action. She contacted the teacher and explained the concerns she had with this depiction of older people. It was too late to cancel the "dress like a 100-year-old" day, but the day after, Papa was invited to come to the school and talk with the kids. She told the kids about her 100-year-old aunt.

The kids couldn't believe Papa knew someone that old and peppered her with questions. She took the questions back to her aunt, who wrote a response to the kids. On a subsequent visit to the school, the class had a video conference with Papa's aunt and experienced a different perspective on being old. The teacher took the lesson one step further. She brought in two jars. In one jar, she placed 5 pennies, and in the other 100 pennies. The kids then talked about how much more value the full jar, representing a 100-year-old, brings. The kids got a valuable lesson that day. And the teacher went on to win an award from the board of education for her efforts.

The actions we take, no matter how small, have a ripple effect on society. One of the most powerful things we can do is take a lesson from people like Sister Imelda and Papa and boldly address ageism when and where we see it.

Label Jars, Not People

As we fight ageism, we must also reject the stereotyping, labeling, and prejudice that exist regarding younger generations. The senior living field has been consumed with learning how to build an effective workforce in a market full of millennial workers. We label millennials as having a poor work ethic and unjustifiably high self-esteem levels. We talk about their obsession with technology. This stereotyping of the young is as inaccurate and limiting as stereotyping of the old.

One summer, I hired a millennial intern who had just graduated from college. My colleagues and I were a bit worried about how it would turn out and how she, being so young and fresh out of school, would adapt to working in an office setting. Would she be texting and snap-chatting on her phone all day? Would she be wearing earbuds while working, unable to interact with the rest of us?

Imagine my surprise when she told me that she'd have to get used to using technology, as she preferred to use a pen and her paper calendar and checklists to manage her time. I had to coax her to use our electronic systems! At the same time this was occurring, our retiring CEO was challenging our organization to adapt newer technologies. He was also the person we all called upon when our IT department was unable to solve a computer problem. Fighting ageism requires that we start seeing people as individuals rather than as part of a homogeneous group based only on age.

Getting Real about Getting Old

People sometimes push back about this reframing of old age, saying that we can't disregard the very real changes and challenges that often come with growing older. That's a valid point. Our bodies *do* change. They *don't* perform the way they did when we were young. There *are* more aches and pains and health concerns. There *are* age-related changes that happen in our brains. There *is* deterioration of hearing and sight. We can't pretend that these things don't exist. But what we *can* do is begin viewing these changes as just one part of the experience, rather than as the defining characteristics of growing old. In youth, our bodies, brains, ears, and eyes may function perfectly, but we are hampered by a lack of experience. In old age, those physical components may change, but we benefit from the knowledge and experience that come only from living many years. Every phase of life comes with gifts and challenges.

It's critical that we spend time evaluating the fears and beliefs we hold about aging. It's important for all of us. As we've learned, the more positive we feel about aging, the better we will age. But it's even more important for those of us who work in the field of aging services. We are in the ideal position to become aware, make a stand, and work toward eliminating ageism and ableism.

Questions for Discussion and Introspection

Ask your team and residents to do an ageism awareness challenge for a week. Where are the ageist messages you're exposed to coming from? How do they impact the way you feel about your own aging process and aging in general?

Do you address ageist messages and conversations when you encounter them? Why or why not?

What fears do you have about growing older? What excites you
about growing older? What are the positive things that come
during the later phases of life?

In what ways are ageism and ableism currently impacting your
organization?

What opportunities are there in your organization to start changing
the conversation about aging? What about in your personal life?

Who in your organization could start working on a plan to address
ageism and ableism?

CHAPTER 4

A Cruel Irony

Ageism, Ableism, and Segregation in Senior Living[1]

RECOGNIZING THE DEVASTATING IMPACT of ageism in our society, in 2016, LeadingAge's president and CEO, Katie Sloan, unveiled the organization's inspirational vision for the future: *an America freed from ageism*. Sloan stressed the critical role that the organization's members—mainly not-for-profit senior living organizations—would play in making this goal a reality. As providers heeded this call to action, many thought it an overwhelming task. After all, how could we change the media, advertising, and our entire nation's view of aging?

In reality, the first steps on this journey start much closer to home.

Before Sloan's new vision was announced, I was part of a LeadingAge Leadership Academy team that was taking steps to understand and address ageism. As my team explored this problem, we quickly realized that, while ageism is a big problem in society, there exists a cruel irony. Retirement communities should be a safe haven from the negativity surrounding old age. But, unfortunately, some of the most blatant examples of ageism and ableism occur in these settings.

In 2015, the *New York Times* ran the story, "An Unexpected Bingo Call: You Can't Play,"[2] which shared the plight of Ann Clinton, an independent living resident in a continuing care retirement community (CCRC), or life plan community, as they are often now called. Clinton had long been a bingo player with other residents of the community. But when she needed to live in the community's skilled nursing center following surgery, she was banned from playing, first by a staff member and then by her fellow residents.

A similar *New York Times* article, written by popular author Jennifer Weiner, entitled "Mean Girls in the Retirement Home,"[3]

describes Weiner's grandmother's (whom she called "Nanna") experience of being rejected in her retirement community dining room and
excluded from bridge games. Weiner surmises that the ostracism of her
grandmother stemmed from ageism. "When you get to be Nanna's age,
you're reduced to a number—the younger the better," Weiner writes.
"Even in a residence for the elderly, the 80-somethings will still be cold
to the 95-year-olds."

Those who work in senior living settings aren't surprised by stories
like this. It's common in a senior living community for residents to
complain about living with old people, ask why so many people with
walkers and wheelchairs are moving in, or shun their neighbors who
are living with dementia. Cliques and bullying are all too common—
and they often stem from prejudice and stereotyping based on an individual's age or physical or cognitive challenges.

This prejudice is internalized by team members as well. We
may hear marketing professionals say that it's impossible to sell a
community to active seniors when there are people in wheelchairs
sitting in the lobby, and some communities may actively "hide" such
residents during tours. I was taught, as many of us were, that when
selling senior living communities, we should never walk prospects
through the nursing home. Even today, frail elders are often hidden away from the rest of the population. When I visit communities with different areas or levels of living, the tour guide generally
avoids the nursing home and has to be asked to show that area of the
community.

The very basic physical and operational structures of many
retirement communities often serve to segregate frail elders from
the rest of the population. Some have policies and operational practices that make it difficult for, or even expressly prohibit, residents of
assisted living or skilled nursing from participating in the dining or
activity programs of the independent living population. Frail elders
who are aging in place within their independent living apartment
homes often experience the pain of being shunned and ostracized by
their neighbors.

Even the budget process may be impacted, with organizations
allocating less money to provide for the dining or programmatic needs
of higher levels of care. I remember touring one beautiful community
and speaking with the dining services director, who was very proud
of his community's focus on ensuring that menu choices were the
same for all residents, no matter where they lived in the community.

I was thrilled, until, as an afterthought, he added, "Of course, we use cheaper cuts of meat in the nursing home."

Pay attention the next time you visit a community with different areas and levels of living. Even in the most beautiful, well-kept communities, a noticeable difference in the décor and maintenance of the nursing home area can often be observed.

As my Leadership Academy team and I began exploring this issue, we realized that if there was one place in society where an elder *should* be accepted and honored, no matter how frail and no matter what challenges he or she is living with, it should be a retirement community.

Many difficult questions began bubbling to the surface. Are we really honoring older people when we focus on and celebrate only those who are well? Where else in society would it be acceptable to segregate and marginalize people who are deemed "undesirable" by their peers? Why was this happening? And, most importantly, what could we do about it?

We began talking with residents and team members at our communities to learn more about their experiences with segregation and prejudice.

We Need to Belong

As discussed in chapter 2, a sense of belonging is a fundamental human need. When an individual experiences social rejection and is marginalized or ostracized, there are devastating results. Unfortunately, this experience is commonplace in many senior living settings. Residents experience this rejection in a variety of ways.

"They [the other residents] seem to be looking at me, but they are really looking over me," explained Helen, an assisted living resident. Sally, a nursing home resident, boldly put herself out there, despite the reactions of "healthy and well" residents. "I go where I want and do what I want. They [meaning the independent living residents] don't like it and that's tough," she said as she stuck out her tongue and laughed. "I am a person! I am not this!" Sally added, pointing to her wheelchair, "I am a person and I have a right to go wherever I want. I have wheels and they have legs, but we are all the same."

Regardless of the circumstances, social acceptance is crucial to self-image. According to Jaya Seenichamy, LCSW, Ph.D., a practitioner who specializes in the mental health needs of elders, an individual's self-image is constantly evolving and developing.[4] "When one's self-image

is negatively impacted, we see rapid decline. When people are ostracized or marginalized, they will compensate in some way," explains
Seenichamy. "Some become aggressive, some self-isolate, some end up
with depression and anxiety."

We usually think of such devastation resulting from years of mis-
treatment and fail to see how occasional whispered comments about
a person's cognitive or physical status or exclusion from a dining table
could have an impact. However, those seemingly harmless interactions
are very dangerous. Research has shown that even a very short-lived
experience of feeling ostracized can have a strong, negative, and long-
lasting impact.

Over five thousand people participated in a Purdue University
study that used Cyberball, an electronic ball toss game.[5] The game
randomly selected participants to be ostracized and left out of the
interactions. The ostracized participants, regardless of personality
type, had a powerful negative reaction to social exclusion after only 2
to 3 minutes—and without ever seeing the other person face-to-face!

Those living with Alzheimer's disease also experience the pain of
ostracism. Seenichamy reminds us that while dementia impacts cognitive abilities, those living with dementia are often very much in tune
with their environment and the way that people interact with them.

We are social creatures, hardwired to be part of a group. Social
inclusion and acceptance are so critical to well-being that the suffering
caused by social rejection is registered in the same part of the brain
as physical pain. Rejection triggers physiological responses that can
increase a person's risk for asthma, arthritis, cardiovascular disease,
and depression.[6] Significant, and potentially life-threatening, damage
is inflicted on those who are marginalized or ostracized in retirement
communities.

So, why does this situation exist? Why would the very communities
that work so hard to honor elders condone this type of culture?

Dementia expert G. Allen Power, M.D., has introduced the rev-
olutionary proposal that people living with dementia should not be
segregated in memory care neighborhoods but, instead, should live
among their peers. In his book *Dementia Beyond Disease: Enhancing
Well-Being, Revised Edition*, Power makes many strong arguments for
this change.[7] However, the biggest stumbling block to integration is a
lack of acceptance by other residents. "There is a stigma," he explains.
"People are afraid of getting Alzheimer's disease, so they avoid those
who are living with it."[8]

Fear of future disease or decline, indeed, seems to be a driving force behind the exclusion of elders living with frailty. Todd D. Nelson, author of *Ageism: Stereotyping and Prejudice against Older Persons*, defines ageism as "prejudice against our feared future self."[9] That's a definition that can especially resonate with people who live and work in retirement communities. As one woman living in the independent living neighborhood of a life plan community described: "It's somewhat depressing to have a care center here. Odds are that I will end up needing to live there, and no one looks forward to that. When you see people with infirmities, you wonder when you'll be one of them.... It keeps it in the forefront of your mind."

In a fascinating study published in *The Gerontologist*, researchers described the challenges met when introducing baby boomers to an existing retirement community of older residents. Interestingly, ageism, in its traditional definition of prejudice against people of a certain age, was not the main root of the divide.[10] Those of advanced age who were still active and ostensibly healthy were readily accepted by the younger residents. Rather, ableism, defined as prejudice against those living with different physical or cognitive abilities, and fear of age-related illness and debilitation, were at play.

This prejudice against the feared future self is so strong that some senior living organizations bow to the expressed wishes of their current and potential customers. This can lead to marketing professionals avoiding the nursing home or requesting that frail elders not be present during tours. Organizations may create or maintain policies or practices that promote continued segregation by specifying who may dine in or participate in programs in different parts of the community.

All of these practices devalue frail elders and strengthen the unhealthy culture of segregation, ageism, and ableism. In fact, when it comes to the avoidance of those living with Alzheimer's, Power believes that part of the stigma of the disease comes from the segregated and less-than-optimal living environments that our society provides for these individuals. Our community structures and systems are, in fact, part of the problem.

A Moral Imperative

As my Leadership Academy team and I interviewed team members about segregation and prejudice in our communities, we spoke with a marketing professional who had been exploring the issue of segregation, ageism, and ableism in her community. She likened the situation to the civil rights movement and had been using that comparison in discussions of the topic with residents. Indeed, there are parallels. In his *Letter from Birmingham Jail*, Dr. Martin Luther King, Jr., described segregation in this way: "Any law that uplifts human personality is just. Any law that degrades human personality is unjust. All segregation statutes are unjust because segregation distorts the soul and damages the personality."[11]

Thought leaders in the field of aging services have made similar comparisons. "Ageism and ableism, like all prejudices, influence the behavior of their victims," says Bill Thomas, M.D., cofounder of The Eden Alternative. "It is our obligation to address ageism and ableism just as we would address sexism or racism."[12]

There's a saying that what we permit, we promote. It's critical that we begin shifting these cultures and create new norms. And leadership must take a strong and unwavering stand, according to Roger Landry, M.D., president of Masterpiece Living and author of *Live Long and Die Short*. "We have a moral imperative to address this issue," he states. "Communities must set clear expectations for a culture of inclusiveness and be unwilling to accept behaviors that marginalize or ostracize others. All it takes is one person to contaminate a culture."[13]

While calls to action from professionals in our field are motivating, even more compelling is this request from Patricia, a woman living in assisted living as part of a life plan community. While she fondly recalled a friend who didn't mind that Patricia had to eat with her hands, she had begun self-isolating. "I am shy about who I eat with because I can't use my fork and spoon," Patricia said. "I sometimes choose to eat alone in the dining room because I know my eating with my hands can be upsetting to some." Patricia called upon her community's leadership to "help us to trust that we will continue to be accepted even when our hands and words stop working, and help us believe that our friends will always be our friends."

Legal Implications

In 2012, a group of residents of a Norfolk, Virginia, life plan community hired an attorney to protest a new policy that banned nursing home and assisted living residents from the independent living dining room and activity programs. The residents, and their attorney, believed that the policy violated the Fair Housing Act and the Americans with Disabilities Act. In 2015, the case was settled with a consent order to ensure that residents with disabilities "are treated equally and that spouses and friends will be able to eat and socialize together."[14]

Similarly, in 2015 a settlement was reached with a Lincolnshire, Illinois, community that had required that residents be able to feed themselves without adaptive eating devices and to exhibit acceptable social behavior. Unacceptable social behavior, according to the community's dining services policy included "food debris on clothing" and "drool, food, and/or liquid seeping from the mouth."[15]

Accommodating the needs of residents living with disabilities can be tricky, says Daniel Sternthal, an attorney specializing in the healthcare and senior living field, "as there are so many issues that may require discussion and each situation can be very unique and fact specific." Sternthal regularly works with clients trying to accommodate the use of motorized scooters. According to Sternthal, "Providers may restrict usage if they have good reason, as long as they have a legitimate basis for such restrictions and complied with their obligations under the law." Other reasons, like refusing admittance because it makes others uncomfortable or could negatively impact marketing efforts, would likely be considered unlawful discrimination.

Imagine a restaurant refusing to serve patrons because they have had a stroke or are living with dementia or are in a wheelchair. It would be unacceptable, and illegal. As the son of one of the Norfolk retirement community residents stated about his father, "I can take him to any restaurant... except the one in the building he paid $600,000 to move into." Sternthal agrees: "It is difficult to imagine a scenario in which a restaurant would be able to legally discriminate against a disabled patron."

The Power of Inclusivity

Some providers have recognized that the status quo is unacceptable and are working to create environments of acceptance. Changing a deeply rooted culture is difficult, but well worth the effort.

When I began my tenure as executive director at Clermont Park, the community culture was rife with segregation, ageism, and ableism. The independent living section of the community was called the Living Center and, unfortunately, the residents there had taken to calling the nursing home the "dying center." The nursing home was connected to the independent living neighborhood by a dark, spooky hallway, complete with stories of the ghost of a former nursing home resident haunting the area in a blue dress. As you can imagine, the hallway didn't get much traffic.

As part of the redevelopment of the community, the haunted hallway was demolished, and the campus was redesigned to create a welcoming town center that would connect all areas of the campus with the goal of creating an inclusive community.

Because the institutional culture was so strong and deeply rooted, change didn't come easily. And there was pushback. During our first inclusive events, some residents and team members asked why the people in wheelchairs from the nursing home were allowed and complained that they were in the way. However, we found many who shared our vision of a culture of inclusivity.

We purposely scheduled what were traditionally "independent living" programs in the nursing home and assisted living activity spaces. This helped to reduce some of the stigma associated with these areas and had the unintended benefit of more fully utilizing our community's common area spaces. We opened up all programs and dining venues to all residents, no matter where they resided. We began encouraging residents to find friends and neighbors with shared passions and to honor each individual instead of pigeonholing people based on their healthcare needs. We began every new resident orientation meeting with a discussion of ageism and ableism and explained the community's passion for inclusivity, and we heeded Thomas's suggestion to communicate that ageism and ableism were as unacceptable in our community as racism or sexism.

Not long after we started our journey of inclusivity, a group of residents went on an "art in the park" outing to a local park. I still have a photo from that event. It didn't matter who had a walker or a wheelchair or was living with dementia. It was a group of people enjoying each other's company, brought together by a shared love of nature and artistic exploration. It was the perfect example of the culture we were trying to create. Moriah Bernhardt, who was the community life director at the time, described the scene perfectly: "Once people started knowing each other as human beings, they stopped defining each other by their disabilities."

The campus transformed to become a *true* community where people with different needs and levels of ability could regularly come together through dining, programs, and outings. It was no longer the paternalistic relationship the community used to see when more "able" residents felt pity for those who were frail. Instead, all residents were equals. The culture of inclusivity became so deeply rooted that residents would educate each other when a discriminatory remark was made or someone wasn't honoring another resident. Residents also requested ongoing educational opportunities so they could better understand and help support their neighbors who are living with challenges, such as Alzheimer's disease.

Judson Park, a life plan community in Des Moines, Washington, has also been very successful in transitioning to an inclusive culture. During an inclusive community dance, team members commented on seeing one of the nursing home residents "moving so gracefully in her wheelchair, even with limitations of movement on one side of her body." A resident of the community's independent living neighborhood had similar thoughts. While she spent very little time on the dance floor, she explained that what made her evening enjoyable was to "watch those residents who live in the nursing home enjoying the music and not being held back by use of mobility aids." By gathering everyone together, regardless of healthcare needs, Judson Park broke down the invisible walls that existed within their community.

Team members can play an integral role in tearing down these barriers. When Helen, a woman who lived in independent living at St. Ann's Community of Rochester, New York, transitioned to the nursing home, she missed having a kitchen where she would host her friends for dinner parties. When St. Ann's team members heard about this, they mobilized to coordinate a series of get-togethers so Helen could once again enjoy being with her friends. They secured funding through an employee-sponsored fund designed to support such resident-directed care needs, and worked with multiple departments to map out the details. Helen has since hosted her friends on multiple occasions. The experience helped her embrace the nursing center as her home and kept her engaged in the larger community. She credited St. Ann's staff with keeping her connected with her friends and the community.

Like Helen, other people living in environments where barriers have been removed have reaped the benefits of creating and maintaining relationships with their friends. "I have continued to deepen my relationships by seeing my friends," said Alice, an assisted living resident who transitioned from independent living at Judson Park. Resident leaders have emerged to show others the way, added Alice,

"I admire my friend.... She treats everyone the same, no matter if they live in independent living or are sick in the nursing home. She is getting to know the people. She is a real leader that brings people together."

In the highly competitive retirement community market, an inclusive culture may also become a competitive niche. At Clermont Park, where we were at first a bit fearful of how prospects would view our inclusive culture, we began proudly communicating our beliefs when people would come for tours. As then Sales and Marketing Director Nicole Chouris-Pollard explained: "When someone is on a tour and comments on wheelchairs or walkers or seeing so many 'old people,' we tell them about this amazing culture and the way that we honor each individual. We tell them they won't find that in most communities. It's become a selling point." The approach worked. During the time of this transition to inclusivity, the community was also selling newly built, entry fee, life care apartment homes, a product generally embraced by a younger, more active older adult. People loved the concept. The community was at 99 percent occupancy within 12 months of opening and stays close to 100 percent occupancy at all times.

Clermont Park has also experienced family members shopping specifically for a community where their loved ones, who would be living in assisted living, would be accepted by the general population and able to use all of the amenities. The competitors lost out because they didn't allow assisted living residents to dine or attend programs with the rest of the community. As more communities become inclusive and begin selling this culture, those with a traditional model of segregation may lose out.

Unfortunately, inclusive cultures are not yet the norm. For some residents and families, it can be a long and difficult journey to find an inclusive and accepting culture. Donna, the daughter of residents of Newbury Court, a life plan community in Concord, Massachusetts, explained how difficult it was for her parents to find a community where they would be accepted. Other communities wanted to be "a showcase where only youthful, healthy seniors were displayed," she said. "People wracked by the tremors of Parkinson's, debilitated by dementia, or simply gnarled by age were made to feel they were an embarrassment—beings unfit to be seen in public."

It is imperative that we challenge the status quo and put an end to cultures in which frail elders are segregated and ostracized. Our communities deserve better. Our residents deserve better.

Creating Inclusivity

Changing the mindset and deeply rooted culture of a retirement community may seem impossible. It isn't. But it does take a firm commitment and hard work.

One of the most important steps toward creating a culture of inclusivity is getting people on board with the vision for an inclusive future. While a solid commitment from leadership is essential, to ensure optimal success, this new vision should not be presented as a mandate by the executive director or a corporate office. Instead, it is best accomplished by having open and honest discussions about segregation, ageism, and ableism.

When I first started this journey, I had no idea what I was doing. But I knew we had to do something. We started out by just implementing change without much input from residents. We learned pretty quickly that open conversation was a far more effective approach for driving sustainable change. We sat down with residents and explained what we saw happening in our community, described the research about the harm that comes from segregation and ostracism, and shared the belief that we had a moral imperative to create a culture in which everyone was accepted and honored. We explained that we couldn't knowingly continue to foster a culture that was harming other people. And then we asked the meeting participants for their thoughts and feedback.

I remember one group meeting in particular. It didn't take long for people to get excited and to get on board. A couple of residents had been school administrators and likened this vision to the work they had undertaken in their careers to create inclusive learning environments for students with developmental challenges. Others recalled personal experiences as victims of racial or sexual discrimination. Still others described how they had taught their own children to be accepting of others. By allowing time for this back and forth dialogue, these sessions, in effect, reminded residents of the people who they want to be. After all, who wants to be a person who does harm to others? These discussions led to resident commitment to this new vision in a way that a mandate never could have.

Over time, with regular communication, the discussions moved past the basic vision and turned naturally toward determining the steps that would ensure this vision became a reality. Residents embraced the definition of ageism as being "prejudice against our feared future selves" and asked for training and education so they could better support their neighbors and friends living with dementia and other challenges. By educating themselves, their fears subsided, and they were naturally more accepting of others.

We began including a very honest discussion of our inclusive culture with potential residents, and new residents, once they moved in, explaining that in our culture, ageism and ableism were no more acceptable than racism or sexism. We made the decision that it was okay to lose prospective residents if this culture didn't appeal to them, though that was a rarity. We also made a very firm commitment to nontolerance of bullying or clique behaviors that excluded or harmed others.

Residents were empowered to educate their neighbors if they did things that were harmful, and we regularly had discussions about specific situations and challenges. When a situation arose in which a resident living in the memory support neighborhood was unable to keep up with the rest of the bridge players due to cognitive challenges, a group of concerned residents got together to find a solution that would honor everyone and ensure that no one felt left out. They started a beginner's bridge club that allowed their neighbor living with dementia to participate successfully in the game with help from the other players. The more experienced players could then continue their game and play at a faster pace. This was a far cry from the old days, when the resident would have been summarily rejected from the group.

Even in the dining room, usually a place of cliques and "this seat is taken" attitudes, inclusivity prevailed. There was a younger woman living in our skilled nursing neighborhood who loved to dine in the bistro-style restaurant in our Town Center, usually frequented by residents of the independent living neighborhood. She was living with a multitude of medical conditions that left her in a specialized wheelchair. Her hands were gnarled with contractures, she had difficulty sitting up straight, and her body would often twitch uncontrollably. In a traditional setting, she would likely have been ostracized. But at Clermont Park, she was a friend to all and was welcomed with calls of "Come, join us!" whenever she entered the dining room. She was known and honored as a person rather than labeled and rejected for her medical conditions.

With focus, determination, and full-community participation, cultures of inclusivity are within our reach. Over time, this culture becomes "just the way we do things around here." Just as the culture change movement has created a new reality for nursing homes, if we become knowledgeable about, and address the issues of ageism, ableism, and segregation, we can create senior living environments that embody the true meaning of the word *community*.

Questions for Discussion and Introspection

Where does segregation or ostracism of those living with different cognitive and physical abilities occur in your community?

When have you experienced feeling ostracized or marginalized in your own life? How did it impact you?

Discuss the definition "ageism against our feared future selves." How much does the fear of the future play into the way people of different cognitive and physical abilities are viewed and treated in your community?

Who in your organization can work to drive inclusivity?

What education is needed in your organization to drive inclusivity?

CHAPTER 5

Becoming Community Builders

ADDRESSING AGEISM, changing our cultures, and creating inclusive places where everyone feels honored requires that we reframe the identity of our organizations. As we discussed in chapter 2, there are significant gaps that the hospitality model doesn't address.

So if not hospitality, then what? What are we? Who are we? What should we strive to become?

The answer is on most of our websites, brochures, and signs in front of our buildings.

We are communities.

In this chapter, we'll explore our organizations in a different light. Not just as communities in name, but as places in which everyone understands that they are part of the whole and accountable for creating a thriving, successful culture.

Rethinking Our Roles

In both the institutional and hospitality model, the framework of senior living has been one of service provision to older adults. Much like any consumer-focused business, we market and sell services to our customers without any expectation of reciprocity.

I've come to believe that under this model, residents become consumers and recipients of the services we provide, rather than seeing themselves as citizens of a community. There is a stark difference, says Peter Block, community builder and author, between being a citizen and being a consumer.[1] Citizens have roles and responsibilities and accountability to the whole. Consumers, on the other hand, relinquish their power, he says. They assume that others are best suited to define and take care of their needs.

Consumers believe that leadership has the answers.

Indeed, the power and accountability for the success of senior living communities generally lie only with the formal leadership employed by the organization. The CEO or executive director is often seen as the one with all the answers and the one who must fix all the problems. This "love of leadership," says Block, limits us. It lets people off the hook, removing accountability from the individual. It leads to an interesting dichotomy—one of dependency and a sense of entitlement.

I spoke with a colleague about this concept, and she made a comparison to what had occurred in a university where she was working.

"We had this incredible group of incoming freshmen who were motivated, capable, and brilliant," she said, "but we had this focus on customer service with them. We did everything for them and took away all of their problems and struggles and didn't expect anything of them. We ruined their capacity to take ownership of their dreams and to be responsible for resolving the issues that got in their way."

She explained that the group of students became apathetic and critical, continually focusing on the negative and looking to college management to fix things. The irony was that most of them were on full scholarships and not paying for their education. The customer service mindset induced a passivity and helplessness that made it difficult for them to take initiative and collaborate with management to address their concerns. Because they were not being challenged to try new things and find their own solutions to problems, they became disengaged and disinterested consumers—a very different picture from the energetic and resourceful young adults who had started out at the beginning of the year.

I'm convinced that similar scenarios occur in senior living and that this consumer focus is at the root of many of the problems we experience. I've been in communities where residents view team members as "the help" and focus on lodging complaints and expecting management to fix everything rather than solving problems together. Because residents aren't accountable to a larger whole, they may behave in ways that undermine the well-being of others. The residents of these communities aren't bad people. They've been rendered helpless consumers.

As cohousing visionary and architect Charles Durrett has said, "Twenty seniors stranded on a desert island would be better at taking care of their most basic needs than the same twenty left isolated or in an institution."[2]

When we romanticize leadership, we undermine the power of everyone else and render them ineffective in meeting their own needs.

How can we create a different reality?

My friend and colleague Jayne Keller often described her role in leading a retirement community as being the mayor of a small town. Her description was somewhat tongue-in-cheek, but Jayne was on to something. If we were to reimagine our organizations as true communities, then the executive director and the leadership team would function in a fashion similar to the local governance of a village.

According to Block, the local government in a community has two roles: (1) to sustain and improve infrastructure and (2) to build the social fabric of community.[3] So to create true communities, rather than seeing ourselves as the ones who create the vision, solve the problems, and drive change, we must begin to view ourselves as social architects whose role is to provide infrastructure and create a culture that encourages residents and team members to identify with and think more like citizens than consumers and to be a part of the solution by identifying and solving their own issues.

A Sense of Community

Have you ever walked into a senior living community where something just feels different?

"I can't explain it," people say, "it just feels different here."

For years, I've tried to define and name that energy, and I think I've figured it out. That feeling is a sense of community. There's a warm welcome when people enter—and it's not a superficial greeting based off a customer service script. The people who work and live there seem to be excited and in sync. They care about each other. The building hums with possibility and relationships and warmth. There's a palpable energy that comes from so many people working together toward a common goal.

I had the opportunity to be part of building such a community during my time at Clermont Park. We went from an institutional, disjointed culture to one of inclusivity and empowerment. We didn't know what we were doing when we started. We experimented and bumbled along and made a lot of mistakes. We learned about community building as we went along. The lessons, for the most part, came from the people who lived there, who had the most experience with community building. All of us, team members and residents, had to change and grow and adopt new roles.

Community-building in senior living requires intention and a shift in thinking and behavior on the part of all involved. Community psychologists teach us that there are four components of a sense of community[4]:

- fulfillment of needs
- membership
- influence
- shared emotional connection

We in the senior living field usually focus solely on fulfillment of needs, which refers to benefits that one expects from being a part of a community. In a senior living community, that could be the services and support that are provided, such as meals, housekeeping, life enrichment programs, and healthcare. Often this is the *only* thing we focus on. It's what we sell and what we use our time and energy to perfect. Fulfillment of needs is important, but we're missing the three other pieces that are equally, if not more, critical.

Membership and Belonging

Did you ever move to a new town as a child? If so, you likely remember how difficult that first day at school was. You walked into the cafeteria and weren't sure of where to sit or who would accept you. You felt vulnerable, alone, and nervous.

These feelings don't just go away as we get older. Many of us continue to experience those feelings when we start a new job or go to a conference where we don't know anyone. These situations are especially awkward and painful when others in attendance seem to know each other and have established subgroups. You become the odd person out.

Many residents have told me that this is what it feels like to move into a retirement community or to live in a community where there are cliques and established groups that aren't open to welcoming new neighbors. It's extremely unsettling and painful, they say, to be surrounded by other people and feel utterly alone.

Membership and belonging are about being known, welcomed, and accepted by other people. In contrast to that painful sense of disconnection, it's the feeling you have when, for example, you're at a networking event walking around among strangers and finally see a group of close colleagues. You know that when you approach the circle they will step aside, open up the circle, and invite you in. Suddenly, rather than being an outsider, you are part of an "us."

Having an "us," however, means having a "them," or those who don't belong. This is what community psychologists call "boundaries." "Us and them" is often thought of as a bad thing, but boundaries are an important, and necessary, part of community. We have to know who is a part of the group and who isn't. The critical thing to focus on in senior living settings is the intentional creation of an "us" that includes everyone who works and lives in that community—people from all levels of living and people who are living with different abilities. This, I've found, requires working with residents and team members to create new norms.

Norms—or standards of behavior—are part of our everyday lives. When we shake hands with a new acquaintance, stand in line at a store, or lower our voices in a library, we're complying with the norms of our society. Norms help us to make sense of the world around us and provide guidance on how to behave in different situations. Norms are usually so strong and deeply ingrained that they become second nature. We don't behave in a house of worship, for example, the way we would in a bar. We don't have to think about it, we just know what to do.

Norms are so strong that they generally don't have to be communicated in a formal fashion. Instead, other people teach us or we just learn by watching the behavior of others. Those who don't conform with those norms face consequences and are often expelled from the group. Norms are powerful because they're generally enforced by peers and peer pressure, rather than formal structures or laws.

When I lived in Hilton Head, South Carolina, attending the PGA golf tournament was a springtime ritual. People referred to it as the biggest walking cocktail party in the world. It was a fun time, but everyone knew that certain behaviors were expected. You could drink your cocktails and talk and laugh, but when the golf marshal held up the "quiet please" sign, you hushed up immediately. And if you didn't, it usually wasn't the marshal who called you out; it was the other fans who would quickly educate you and put you in your place. If you didn't comply, you'd be asked to leave. With few exceptions, everyone acted within these norms, because they wanted to be included.

Every single day, everywhere we go, we function within the norms of society and the groups we're a part of. We're socialized to expect and respond to norms, but for some reason we shy away from driving the creation and maintenance of healthy norms in senior living settings.

This missing piece, I firmly believe, is what leads to the prevalence of cliques and bullying.

We're reticent to drive healthy norms because of the way we view our roles. Throughout my career, operating from the perspective of a customer service provider, I never talked about norms. I was taught the golden rule of customer service, that the customer is always right, and I felt awkward approaching a resident who was acting in a way that was hurting or disrupting other people or the community. My role, I thought, was to view everyone as my customers and to make sure they were happy.

But when I shifted my thinking, to seeing residents as citizens and myself as a community builder, it changed everything. I realized that I had an absolute obligation to address anything that was doing harm to others or damaging the culture. And, more importantly, I had a responsibility to be proactive in working with residents and team members to create norms that fostered a healthy culture of community and inclusion.

As I shared in chapter 4, before we began our inclusivity work at Clermont Park, we struggled as many communities do. We had resident cliques, bullying, and ostracism of those deemed "less desirable." During meals, residents would dine with the same people every day and become upset when someone new would try to sit at their table. I have talked with many organizations who believe this is just the way it is and that it can't be changed.

But it can.

At Clermont Park, the residents developed new norms of welcoming, which included purposely sitting with different people at mealtimes each day. We created norms of acceptance and inclusion of people living with different cognitive and physical abilities. Just as we don't have to think about standing in line at a store, these norms became second nature and a part of how things were done. Anyone who stepped outside of those norms, for example, by ostracizing or showing prejudice against another resident, was quickly reeducated by the others. If that didn't fix the problem, it became my responsibility to step in—but that rarely happened.

The problem was never the residents. The problem was our culture. When we focus on community, creating healthy norms and a sense of citizenship, people behave differently.

These same healthy norms are in place at Holly Creek, a sister community to Clermont Park. When my parents moved in, they quickly noticed something happening, something much different than the resort culture they had encountered during their tours of other communities.

From the day they moved in, they were welcomed by other residents. Each night they were invited to dinner by different people. Folks would call them or leave notes on their door asking them to join. The people inviting them weren't members of an official welcoming committee. Rather, this practice was embedded deep in the culture. Inclusion and acceptance are simply a part of the social fabric. It has become "just the way we do things around here."

Soon after they got settled, my parents, indoctrinated to the norms, began inviting new residents and those who might be lonely to dinner, thereby strengthening the culture and further spreading these norms.

Influence

A sense of community also requires that members have influence. People need to feel that they matter, that they're a part of something, and that they have an impact on their community.

Creating cultures of influence requires a significant shift in the way we approach decision making in our organizations. In my many years as an executive director operating under a hospitality and customer service framework, I believed that it was the responsibility of management to own and fix every problem. Indeed, that credo of "own the problem" is often taught in customer service training programs.

I tried to involve residents in my decision making. I'd ask them for input on a decision or problem I was facing and would gather their thoughts. Then I'd make the decision and report back to them. I've learned that isn't enough.

Input is *not* the same as influence.

Influence is more than choosing the gray paint or the blue paint or voting on options. It's putting *real* power into people's hands. It's being transparent about problems and owning things together as a community.

This was a tough concept for me to grasp and begin to practice. I was so stuck in my service provider mentality that I had to fight the urge to own every problem.

One day, however, the need to change became crystal clear.

We had been having a lot of issues and complaints about the fairly large population of dogs living at Clermont Park. A resident had come to see me to complain about her neighbor's barking dog. Following my standard protocol, I told the resident I would handle the problem and invited the offending dog's owner to my office to talk about the issue. The dog owner walked in, head hanging, and said, "I feel like I've been called to the principal's office."

That statement hit me hard. I suddenly realized that in my community (and in most communities), residents are relegated to places of lower power than the 40-year-old who runs their community. It's horrible. But that's exactly what happens!

Highly competent, highly experienced human beings move into a senior living setting and become helpless consumers. I realized that on a daily basis people with decades more experience than I were expecting me to solve every issue and address every problem. And often they were small things, things that certainly, after spending so many years on this Earth, they themselves knew how to fix, like talking with a neighbor about their barking dog. I realized that my current approach was undermining the power and capabilities of the people who lived in my community. I was creating helplessness.

So the next time I encountered a dog complaint, rather than offering to "own" the problem or pulling out the pet policy and sending a threatening letter to the offending resident, I called together the pet owners in the building for a meeting. I laid it all on the table and asked not for their input but for their participation and accountability in resolving the rift that had occurred in the community. We talked about the importance of pets and the importance of living in harmony with other residents.

The group decided to start a pet committee that would put in place guidelines for ownership, resources for pet owners, and a structure for dealing with issues. My team and I worked with the group and got the committee started. The goal was to give back their power, get them set up for success, and then get out of their way.

One of the first items the committee tackled was where dogs would be allowed in the building. The old policy, written by management without resident input, stated that dogs were not allowed in common areas. Owners could only go directly from their apartment home to the outdoors, no stopping or sitting and chatting anywhere in the building. This rule didn't seem appropriate for a community that purported to recognize the importance of animal companionship. The committee started talking with other residents. As it turned out, many residents, including those that didn't own pets, liked dogs and didn't mind having them around. Those who didn't like dogs still respected the importance of animals in the lives of pet owners and wanted to support that.

With this input, the committee developed a new policy proposal stating that dogs were welcome anywhere in the building, except dining areas (which would still welcome service animals, of course). Dog owners, however, were expected to hold themselves to a higher standard and to respect those who may not want dogs around. If pet owners wanted to bring their dog to a program, for example, they agreed to ask if others would mind their dog being there. If there was anyone who preferred to have a dog-free zone, the owner would remove the dog. It wasn't perfect—nothing ever is. But residents were able to work through the normal problems that happen when living in a community with pets. They didn't need me to fix everything, and when my team and I got out of the way, better, and more sustainable, solutions were created.

The group then went on to develop systems and structures to support each other and create a healthier community. If someone had a dog that was misbehaving, the group would work together to help train the dog or find training resources. If a resident was ill or otherwise unable to walk the dog, other committee members would jump in and help.

They started "Yappy Hours," where dogs could play together while owners socialized. They organized memorial services when a beloved pet died. And in one very difficult situation, when a resident was almost forced to give up her beloved but aggressive service dog, the committee set up a socialization plan so the dog could learn to behave properly in a safe setting. These successes would never have occurred with the old model of thinking. When people have the opportunity for influence and start thinking of themselves as citizens instead of consumers, they take responsibility for making the community stronger and healthier.

This way of thinking spread to other areas of the community. It became standard practice to convene a group of team members and residents to solve community challenges as they arose. If someone came forward with a complaint, our first question would be, "Would you like to get a group together to work on this?"

We got rid of the old management-imposed dress code in the formal dining room, and residents did the hard work of coming to a solution that would honor the upscale feel of the dining room but not exclude family members and others who may prefer to wear jeans and be more casual. When residents expressed dissatisfaction with the transportation program, we got a group together, shared the budgeted number of hours and other logistical items involved with running a transportation program, and worked together to come up with a new solution that worked both logistically and financially.

This new way of thinking also began to impact our marketing messages. Instead of just focusing on what we "do" for residents, we started asking new questions like, "What talents, skills, and passions will you bring if you move in? How do you want to share these gifts to make the community stronger and more vibrant?"

We have an incredible resource in our communities—people with vast amounts of experience and knowledge. When we promote influence and encourage experience and knowledge to play out in community decision making, we achieve much better outcomes. Outcomes are also much more readily accepted. Every time we convened a group to work on a problem, we opened it up to anyone who was interested in participating and said, "If you aren't a part of developing the solution, you forfeit your right to complain about the outcome."

A sense of community requires that influence is bi-directional. In addition to *having* influence, community members must also be influenced *by* the community. One day, not long after my parents moved into Holly Creek, my dad, who's on the younger and more active side of the typical resident, said something profound: "Living in this community is making me a better person." He explained that Holly Creek's culture of acceptance and inclusivity had helped him to move past the internalized ageism and ableism that we all experience, and to see past a person's walker or wheelchair and frailty and really know the human being. He was having so much fun learning from and getting to know people who were in their 90s and 100s. It brought richness and wisdom into his life. The culture of inclusivity has become so important to him that he's now heading up a committee that is working to drive more inclusion for residents who live in assisted living and the nursing home.

This is what we should strive to become—communities that promote bi-directional influence and help the community, and everyone in it, to grow.

Shared Emotional Connection

Shared emotional connection is often viewed as one of the most important components of creating a sense of community. It's about encouraging real relationships where community members experience meaningful interactions and emotional risk with each other. It is *the* marker of a true community.

While we often think that we're creating a community when we bring together people with shared interests and values and location of residence, we've really only convened a group. True community, says Charles Vogl, author of *The Art of Community: Seven Principles for Belonging*, comes only when people are connected to and care for each other.[5]

I've come to realize that many of the things I've done throughout my career undermined the opportunity to build those shared emotional connections. The approach I took to problem solving, for example, of having residents come to me with conflicts they were having with other residents, disempowered people and undermined the connection and understanding that comes when two people work through a difficult situation together.

As we moved through our journey of community building, we began to tap into that opportunity and to use tools that were typically employed with team members—such as personality assessments and conflict resolution training—in educational programs with residents so they could work together to resolve issues.

Even more damaging than my decision-making style was the way I approached very difficult times in our community, such as the loss of a resident. There is a strong bonding experience that occurs when a group of people goes through a difficult emotional time or crisis together; if you've ever gone through a traumatic or trying time with a group of people, you know what I mean. Supporting each other through tough times brings us closer together.

As we discussed in chapter 2, when we use a hospitality approach in our communities, we tend to create visions of shiny, happy places— like Disney World—where unpleasant things happen only behind the scenes, in the back-of-house areas. In front of our customers, when we're "on stage," we're encouraged to create a pristine, trouble-free experience.

This is the approach I used in handling resident deaths for many years. From the time I entered the field, I was taught that people don't want to see death or anything that reminds them of death. So, as is the case in many communities, when someone would die, I would hide it as much as possible.

My team and I would close all of the other resident doors. The undertaker would come, put the covered body on a stretcher, and take it out the back door, where the hearse would be waiting. We would then record a reduction in census on our census tracking form, pack up the person's belongings in plastic trash bags for the family to pick up, and move on to find a new occupant for the room. Once a month, we'd hold a memorial service to recognize all the people who had died that month. It was cold and inhumane and nothing like the way we handle death in "regular" life, where healing rituals and mourning occur.

This is the way I operated in my buildings for the first 10 years of my career. I'm ashamed to admit this, but I never questioned it. I never asked the people who lived and worked in my community what they thought or what they wanted. I believed I was acting in their best interest—no one wants to face the grim fact of death, right?

It wasn't until I went to a Certified Eden Associate Training that I was introduced to a new approach. I learned about communities that were handling things differently: they didn't just acknowledge death, they embraced it as a part of life. There were community-driven rituals in place. There was emotional bonding occurring.

At the time, I was a nursing home administrator and the home where I worked had been hiding death for many years. I went back to the nursing home and sat down with a group of residents. I explained to them what I had learned and how we currently removed bodies through the loading dock door. I asked them for their thoughts and feelings about our current approach.

It was painful to hear their responses.

"It's not okay to take the person out the back door," said one woman. "That's where the trash goes."

"It's horrible the way we do this," said another. "I don't know that a friend has died until I see an empty seat at the lunch table."

Another said she wanted to know when someone died, even if she didn't know the person, because she wanted to pray for the person. "What if no one else is praying for them?" she asked with tears in her eyes.

They were so passionate with these views that I was startled.

Why had no one spoken up before?

The answer, I now understand, is that it wasn't a true community. The culture, as exists in many nursing homes, was so dysfunctional that residents were disconnected from each other and the larger whole. And worse, they were never empowered to question the status quo or raise their concerns.

When I began working at Clermont Park, I found the same practices in play—the back door exit, the lack of communication, the lack of community-driven rituals and opportunities to mourn. Our approach was out of alignment with the culture of respect and dignity that we were striving for.

Our chaplain started having discussions with residents throughout different areas of the campus.

The same themes arose.

"I'm almost 90," one resident said. "Do you think I don't know that people die? Why are you trying to pretend it doesn't happen?"

Another said that because we weren't honoring death, we weren't honoring life and those who are living. Shuffling a body out the back door sends a strong message about the value we placed on the people who lived in the community. "How can you say this community values us," she said, "when you treat us this way when we die?"

We also talked with team members. They shared with us the devastation they feel when someone passes away. Regardless of position, those of us who work in communities feel deep pain when a resident dies. Team members, such as nursing assistants, who help residents eat, get dressed, and bathe, often have even deeper and more intimate relationships.

"Do you know how it feels," asked one team member, "to have known and loved a resident for years and then be off for a couple of days and come back and find that the person has died? No one called me. I just have to go back to work and pretend that everything is okay."

Think about how the death of a friend or family member is handled in "regular" life. You would be called, even in the middle of the night, with the news. You would gather together with family and friends to talk and mourn the loss. You would cook food and rally around the family members of the deceased. Depending on your religion and beliefs, you would sit shiva, attend a funeral, or participate in other rituals.

The extreme dysfunction and damaging effects of our institutional approach quickly became evident.

Our community started working together to bring back normal and healthy rituals following the loss of a community member. This wasn't something that was written in a policy or declared by our chaplain team. It was developed by residents and those who work most closely with them.

It started with residents sharing their wishes for their passing, how they wanted to be remembered, and how they wanted to say goodbye to their friends. If a resident was dying and wanted friends and team members to be notified, we let them know that it was time to say goodbye. (For those of you who are concerned about HIPAA violations, see chapters 8 and 10 for a discussion about a concept called surplus safety.)

Then, when the person passed away, if the resident had wished, everyone would be notified when the undertaker had come. Everyone who wished to participate would line up in the hallway for a processional and walk out the front door of the building with the body to the hearse. We'd often sing "Amazing Grace" or the resident's favorite song. Then, according to the resident's wishes, a meaningful and very personalized celebration-of-life service was held for all to attend. These were the most beautiful, meaningful, cathartic rituals I've ever been a part of.

Because this new approach wasn't a policy or procedure mandated by management, it had meaning to everyone and happened naturally at any time—whether it was 2:00 in the afternoon or 2:00 in the morning. Team members also developed informal networks to inform those who weren't working when someone had passed away and would also sometimes come together in informal learning circles to talk about their feelings. Different team members found their own special ways to honor people. One nurse, using the principles of feng shui, would rearrange a dying resident's room, if he or she wished. She'd play soothing music and place meaningful items, such as family photographs, within easy reach and sight of the resident.

When we first started this journey to normalize death, many in the community thought it would only apply in the nursing home. Residents in independent living, they said, are in a different place in their lives and wouldn't want to think about death.

That, as with most assumptions, was wrong. Residents and team members throughout the community began implementing new rituals and processes.

By fostering a healthy and respectful approach to death, the entire culture shifted. Two years after I left Clermont Park, Ronnie Brown, the executive director, let me know that a resident with whom I had been close had passed away. I was invited to her celebration of life ceremony, which had been entirely planned by the resident and her friends. It was originally to be a combination 94th birthday and bon voyage party. She had been in hospice and wanted the party to be a celebration as she left this Earth for her next great adventure.

"If I die before the party," she had said, "make it a celebration of my life." And it was.

The room was packed with family, friends, and team members. All were asked to bring red wine or dark chocolate. The celebration was full of laughs and stories. People came together to share their grief and their happy memories.

When we sanitize life and try to hide everything that might feel uncomfortable, we devalue the people who live and work in our organization and create unhealthy environments. When we are open and embrace the bad and the good in life, we build community as people come together to work through the hard times.

It's Never Too Early to Build Community

At Clermont Park, we created community through mistakes and failures and experimentation. I always wondered if it was a fluke—a compilation of the right people at the right time—or if it could be replicated. When I was promoted to a new role with multisite responsibility opening new buildings, I looked for executive directors who understood the sense of community we had created and taught them some of the lessons I had learned and mistakes I had made.

This culture of community, I learned, can happen everywhere. And it can happen much more quickly than I thought.

I visited Cappella of Grand Junction, an assisted living community, a few months after it had opened and attended a resident council meeting. I settled into my chair, expecting to hear the usual complaints about a new building, how systems and processes weren't yet working well and how there were many hiccups in services.

Owen Ash, the resident council president, opened the meeting.

"Let's start the meeting by discussing what's going well," he said.

My mouth dropped open. This isn't how resident council meetings usually go!

The residents began sharing their excitement about how good the food had been and what a great job the team members had been doing. But what shocked me the most was that the majority of the conversation centered around the feeling of community that had already begun to flourish. These new residents owned the success of the community and its culture. They talked about how much everyone cared for each other. They talked about the close friendships that had already been made. They discussed their role as residents in the community as coming together, solving problems, and making it a better place. These folks weren't passive consumers of services. They were citizens!

I sat down with Ash and the executive director, Sarah Winnefeld, after the meeting to ask how they had built such a strong community in a matter of months. Winnefield explained that she had a very clear vision of the culture of community that she was trying to build. When she met Ash, she saw that he had the leadership qualities that could help her realize that vision.

Ash and Winnefield work together to look for acts of kindness between residents and team members and recognize those acts. They encourage team members to dine with residents and encourage residents to sit with different people at every meal. Ash explained that when residents move into a community, they're terrified. The world, he said, tends to categorize people and label them. To fight that tendency, he explained, people need to get to know each other and understand that they have an important role to play. "We all come here with challenges we're dealing with," he said, "but we don't let that define us. We're a community here, and we all have important roles to play."

Questions for Discussion and Introspection

How does the role of community builder or social architect differ from the way you currently view your job responsibilities? What changes would you need to make to adopt a new approach?

What norms (healthy or unhealthy) currently exist in your community? Are new residents (and team members) welcomed through well-established norms of inclusivity?

How can you create healthy norms to build membership and a sense of belonging?

In what situations do residents and team members have true influence (not just input) in the community? How can this be expanded?

How do you currently handle difficult situations, such as the death of a resident? Are there community-driven rituals in place? What do you think about your current practices? How are they impacting the community?

Who in your organization could start driving a focus on community building?

CHAPTER 6

Old Dogs and New Tricks

Creating Cultures of Possibilities and Growth

REFRAMING OUR ORGANIZATIONS as true communities—giving people opportunities for influence, belonging, and shared emotional connection—requires that each person grow and learn in order to take on a new identity and role. This can be a challenge. The ageist messages of our society often lead us to believe that, as the old adage says, "you can't teach an old dog new tricks." In this chapter we'll explore opportunities to challenge the false assumption that growth stops at a certain age and create, instead, a culture of possibilities and growth.

Rooted in the Past

Growth and learning are central themes throughout most of our lives. As children, people ask us what we want to be when we grow up. In our teen years, we're asked where we want to go to college. During early and mid-adulthood, we're always working toward some future growth opportunity—raising a family, finishing a degree, working toward a promotion, learning a new skill.

But then, as we enter elderhood, society no longer expects us to grow. The belief that older people can't learn still limits many of us, despite recent research on brain plasticity that shows the brain can create new connections throughout life.

While we may want to believe that we've overcome these beliefs in senior living settings, many of the things we do are evidence that this negative stereotype remains very much a part of our thought processes. In many places, I've seen too often that from the moment we begin interacting with potential residents, we send the message that their identity and value is rooted in the past. Rather than focusing on the future, our discussions and paperwork usually focus on what a person's career was, what hobbies they enjoyed, how many kids they raised, and where they grew up. We share that information in resident biographies, and in many communities it informs our programming plans.

Rather than encouraging people to, as Dr. Kathleen Taylor of St. Mary's College says, "jiggle their synapses a bit by challenging long-held assumptions and beliefs,"[1] we often frame elders as static beings with static belief systems. "He's 90 years old," we'll say. "He's been racist his whole life. He'll never change his views." Rarely do we challenge people to adopt, as we discussed in the last chapter, new norms or behaviors. Our calendars are often full of nostalgia—music and movies from decades ago—rather than forays into the contemporary. And if you've ever tried to jazz up a menu with new culinary features, you've likely had someone say to you, "These people like meat and potatoes. You'll never get them to change."

It's important that we shift this paradigm. Of course, personal history is important. We're shaped by the lives we've lived and the experiences we've had. History can also help us find common connections with each other. But identifying people as only who they were in the past is limiting and, too often, it defines our cultures and environments. Learning new things, and exercising our brains with unfamiliar and challenging concepts, is critical to maintaining cognitive health as we age.[2] Learning may take a little more time than when we're younger, but the older brain *can* learn new things and continue to grow.[3]

Whom Will You Become?

At Clermont Park, our association with The Eden Alternative and Masterpiece Living led us to challenge our view of residents as stagnant beings whose identity was rooted in the past. The philosophies of both organizations promote growth and learning for everyone. Masterpiece Living, in particular, focuses on encouraging people to go outside their normal ruts of thinking and behavior in order to sustain brain health and grow new brain synapses. Masterpiece Living initiatives, such as the Living It! Campaign, encourage residents to try new and unfamiliar things.

When we started driving this new culture of exploration, we encountered resistance. One day, Moriah Bernhardt, the campus community life director, and I were talking about some of the struggles we were having in eliminating the status quo of stagnation. Why were so many residents so stuck in the past and afraid to change? Bernhardt had an insight. "We're always asking who people were," she said. "Why aren't we asking whom they want to become?" We realized that, from day one, our whole approach and culture were sending limiting messages to residents rather than promoting an evolving sense of self. We were promulgating the negative myths of aging, right in our own community!

We started asking different questions. Whom will you become? What do you want to learn? How do you want to grow? At first, people thought we were crazy. Residents and prospective residents were so unfamiliar with anyone asking questions about growth and learning in our community that it caught them off guard.

"What do you mean, what's next for me?" some asked, suspiciously.

It made people uncomfortable at first. But we kept pushing. And a new culture of growth was sparked.

Tackling Technology

One of the first initiatives we embarked on was bringing technology to the community. We had been searching for a new solution to the daily check-in process at our community. A system of check-in is common in independent living settings; it's a way to ensure that someone hasn't fallen, alone in their apartment, in need of help without anyone knowing.

Our existing system worked like this: Each resident had a crocheted ring. Before going to bed, residents would hang the ring on their doorknob. A staff member or volunteer would then walk the building during the night and check all the doors. A bare doorknob indicated that the resident may have fallen or was otherwise incapacitated. We would knock on the door and make sure the person was okay. In the morning, the process would be reversed—the resident would take the ring in and a volunteer or staff member would walk the halls and look for any rings still hanging on the doorknob.

The system was decidedly low tech and labor intensive. And, as is any process that is completely dependent on people, it was also prone to human error, which was creating some risk management concerns.

We identified a new system—a touchscreen tablet, with a special application installed, for each apartment home. This technology was the answer to a lot of our problems. Each morning the resident would be electronically prompted to tap the tablet to indicate that he or she was up and okay. A list of anyone who hadn't checked in would be automatically emailed to the concierge, who could then call the resident and, if needed, go to the apartment to make sure all was well. In addition to ease of use and efficiency, the tablets also offered other great features. Calendars, menus, messaging to team members, and other community information would be available on the tablets, right at residents' fingertips.

I was thrilled, but not everyone was. A lot of residents were very upset. With an average age of around 85, and some residents who were more than 100 years old, most living in the community had never used a computer before. When they wound down their working careers in the late '70s or early '80s, the Sony Walkman and the microwave oven were new and exciting technologies. After retiring, several people told me they had stopped keeping up with new inventions, and computers just hadn't been a part of their lives.

As a result, when we introduced the concept of eliminating the crocheted rings in favor of a tablet in each apartment, it didn't go well. In fact, I learned later on that a Pew Research Center study found that more than half of older adults who were not currently using the Internet didn't believe that technology could be relevant in their lives,[4] a view many of the residents in our community held. Many also doubted their ability to learn new skills and were overwhelmed by the coming change. When a volunteer learned about our plans, she admonished me for forcing technology on those "poor old souls."

Fortunately, within the larger culture of trepidation, we found a small group of residents who were excited about the possibilities of this new technology. Some of them were already comfortable with computers. Others were just intrigued with the idea of trying something new. This group became our technology leaders. They participated in a pilot program with the beta version of the application and gave feedback to the programmers. As they tried out the tablets, they started enjoying the new app and exploring outside of it, trying out social media sites and the myriad other tools and resources available on the Internet. They also began talking with their neighbors about the fun they were having.

Still, when we were ready to roll out the system to the entire community, there was much anxiety.

We set up numerous classes for residents to get their tablets and learn how to use them in a classroom setting. But we made a critical error during that first phase of implementation. Because we were still trapped within our ageist framework, we thought that one of our team members in her early 20s would be the best person to teach the residents—after all, who better to teach technology than a millennial who had been using it since childhood?

Our team member's experience ended up being a detriment. Because she was so comfortable with technology, we didn't anticipate some basic problems that would arise. We didn't understand that we would have to teach the basics, such as how to turn on the tablets. We didn't anticipate how daunting touchscreen technology could be, or that we'd have to teach people the proper way to "tap" the screen and get a stylus for each person to make the "tapping" easier. We also didn't understand the educational approach that was needed. We had been trying to teach residents by having them sit in a classroom with a tablet in front of them, following along with the instructor.

And then Mary Johnson, a retired educator and resident, saw what we were doing wrong. She stepped up and offered to help, and we quickly realized she could teach this new technology much better than we ever could.

Mary understood that teaching the residents how to use a tablet *on* the actual tablet wasn't working. She created poster boards of screenshots from the tablet and taught the concepts first on paper, something her students were used to and comfortable with. Once they had learned in a more familiar and comfortable manner, she then moved them to the tablets.

Mary took over the training program, educating more than two hundred residents. One year after implementation, 95 percent of residents were using their tablets to check in on a daily basis (for those unable to use the technology, alternate solutions were put into place). They also started using the tablets for other things. One resident, an avid watercolor painter, began using her tablet to look up photographs of flowers she could reference while painting. Others began Skyping with their families and friends, joining social media, and exploring the Internet. One of the most vocal opponents of the tablets completely shifted her attitude after she learned how to use it and started helping to problem solve use of the tablet with a friend with low vision. Together they came up with tactile cues that enabled her friend to operate the tablet.

The tablets opened up new worlds for people. The experience of overcoming fear and learning something new was like a shot of energy in the community. As one resident told me, "Once we learned how to use the tablets, we realized we could do and learn anything."

A New Culture of Growth

Following the successful tablet implementation, things started to shift. We started to see people trying new things and pushing outside their boundaries. This spirit of innovation started with a small group and spread throughout the community. Rather than sticking with the familiar, residents were seeking challenges that would stretch them and help them to grow.

A new culture of acceptance was created. People suddenly became more comfortable with making mistakes and even looking foolish as they learned new things. It was amazing to walk by the fitness center in the morning and see men who I thought were "buttoned up" serious types trying silly dance moves in exercise class.

Every day, it seemed, someone was trying something new. Our fine arts studio, which in the past would have been called an "arts and crafts room," became a place of exploration and creativity. One resident had been a mathematician all his life and had never explored the arts. He had always wanted to try pottery. Once he got his hands on the clay, he was hooked. He became one of our most celebrated potters. Others learned to paint and draw or quilt. We found an unused hallway and created a resident-run art gallery where people could display their newfound talent.

One resident decided that she wanted to do things that thrilled and scared her. She went sky diving, zip lining, and diving with the sharks at an aquarium, all during the year that she turned 90. Others started taking Spanish classes. Some learned to write poetry. Still others learned how to line dance. While our community had once been quite conservative and limited in its religious leanings, residents began exploring other religions of the world and new ways of thinking.

Sparked by a team member who was active in the performing arts, residents also decided to try their hand at producing a musical. For the vast majority of cast members, this was their first experience with acting and singing in front of other people. The production was open to all residents, no matter where they lived in the community and no matter what their abilities. It has become an annual event with wide participation, selling out multiple performances each year.

Everyone had opportunities to share and grow in the production of these musicals. An assisted living resident who was living with dementia led the creation and painting of scenery, teaching others how to paint in the process. A resident from the nursing home took charge of costumes. And the cast included anyone who wanted to participate. Residents created modified costumes for people needing wheelchairs and walkers.

Some residents living with dementia also participated as cast members. In the beginning, we worried that they wouldn't be able to learn their lines. What we found was astounding. Those who, in the beginning, couldn't remember to get to rehearsals improved significantly. By show time, they not only remembered every rehearsal, but also had memorized all their lines.

Educational Initiatives

As the culture of growth deepened and strengthened, residents started feeling more comfortable talking about their ideas and dreams. In 2013, resident Elsa Wycisk spoke with Bernhardt about how much she was enjoying learning and trying new things in such a vibrant atmosphere. "It's just like a college," said Wycisk, "except we can't get degrees. I wish we could get a degree here."

Bernhardt didn't just chuckle about the comment and move on. She thought, "What if we *could* be a college? What would that look like?" She and Wycisk got a group of residents together to talk about the idea. After months of dreaming and discussing the vision, the group in 2014 launched Clermont College of Creative Life. The college is an entirely resident-driven initiative focused on growth, creativity, and exploration.

Classes are taught and attended by residents, family members, team members, volunteers, and individuals from the surrounding community. The college operates on a tri-semester basis, each with a different focus area, such as social justice or healthy living. Through a partnership with the University of Denver, students in the Graduate School of Social Work attend and participate in teaching classes at Clermont Park. Topics run the gamut from studying Hebrew, learning about quality improvement, and creating botanical illustrations to navigating the stock market and practicing forgiveness. The focus of the college is stretching people outside of their comfort zones, which results from not only attending classes but also teaching them. For many residents and team members who are fearful of public speaking, the college offers a safe environment to overcome that fear and hone their presentation skills.

To graduate, participants must take thirty courses throughout the year, including ten credits focused on personal growth and exploration. To date, 164 residents and team members from across the levels of living on campus have graduated from the college. Formal leadership from throughout the entire organization is highly engaged and involved. The former CEO, for example, taught a class in beer making, and the human resources team taught classes on interviewing skills to prepare residents to participate in the selection process for new team members.

In 2015, Clermont College of Creative Life was awarded the International Council on Successful Aging's Innovators Achievement Award. When interviewed by the *Journal on Active Aging*, a staff member said the main problem the community was facing was having more instructors than they could use each semester![5]

At Judson Park, a HumanGood community in Des Moines, Washington, Executive Director Nikole Jay embarked on a similar initiative. As part of their Masterpiece Living journey, Jay convened a group of resident leaders to discuss how they could enhance intellectual well-being in the community. The group talked about what intellectual growth meant to them and how they wanted to grow that aspect of their community. As at Clermont Park, what sprung from that discussion was the creation of a new educational initiative, which Judson Park residents named The College of Intellectual Inspiration.

The resident-led college started small but quickly grew in size and scope. Resident connections led to opportunities to learn from visiting scholars, such as the Dalai Lama's physician. The college has a strong focus on social issues and the function of government. College participants provide support to local community service organizations and serve as mentors and career coaches for local high school students. According to Jay, about 330 people live at Judson Park, and every class is overflowing with as many as 120 participants. At the time of this writing, the college is making plans to open up its educational offerings to the public.

Personal Growth and Transformation

The key to instilling a culture of growth is ensuring that residents drive the process and understand how the things that they're learning can impact their lives. When team members at Casey's Pond Senior Living began a healthy aging education initiative, they struggled to get residents engaged. Residents didn't believe they could change or learn at their advanced age. They also doubted that lifestyle adjustments could really have an impact late in the life span.

However, when a group of residents read a book about the ways that lifestyle impacts the brain and cognition, it clicked for them. They realized that they could impact their well-being at any age and embarked on an 8-week class to study lifestyle changes. "Knowing they had some control over the rest of their years got them out of their ruts," explains Cathy Reese, Lifestyle Director. The group started exploring everything from dietary changes to the Japanese practice of forest bathing, which encourages mindful interactions with nature. Once the group saw how their lives were changing, they began challenging others, including team members, to join them on their quest for better health.

This belief that people can grow at any age is absolutely critical to well-being. As our circumstances and bodies change over our life span, we *must* learn and grow and adapt. Too often, people believe they can't learn a new skill or adaptation and decide to give up, which leads to further deterioration.

With a mindset of stagnation, for example, my mom, with her vision loss, wouldn't be able to function and would become completely dependent on others. Adapting to blindness requires significant learning and growth. Because she believes she can learn new things, and lives in a community that promotes exploration, she's learned to navigate her building and explore the walking trails in the neighborhood. She also stayed for a week at the Colorado Center for the Blind's Seniors in Charge program. There, my mom explains, she and other participants were challenged to go beyond the tragedy of blindness and learn the skills needed to live a full and engaged life. I attended the closing ceremony of this program and learned from participants how their lives had expanded and flourished as a result of gaining a new perspective and skill set. As one participant said, "It's hard to summarize this experience. How can words describe something so profound?"

Continued growth and transformation aren't just about developing a college or a formal training program. Sometimes it can be the small things. Jim Kok, who oversees chaplain services for Christian Living Communities and serves as the chaplain at Holly Creek, where my folks live, believes that in addition to supporting people where they are in their lives, his role is to help people grow.

Often, that means he's a mirror for their behavior.

We've all known a crabby resident, someone who is rude or aggressive or offensive. Too often we ignore it and say, "that's just how he is," and try to turn the corner when we see that person coming down the hall. Kok, however, takes a different approach. He believes that everyone can grow. He has no qualms about saying to the person, "You're being that stereotypical grouchy old guy. You're being unkind to people. Is that who you want to be?" He calls it having a "your fly is open" conversation—caring enough to help someone understand how they're being perceived by others. Kok then engages the person in a discussion about what's going on and how that person may want to adjust his or her approach to others. Usually, he says, the person will respond, think about how he or she is acting, and adapt his or her interactions.

There's another surprising benefit of focusing on continued growth as we age. Learning new things may also address one of the very common and troubling experiences of old age—the perception that time has sped up.

"Where did the time go?" many of us ask, as we puzzle over children who have seemingly grown up overnight or a year that has passed by in what seems a few months. It seems that the older we get, the faster time passes. As it turns out, scientists believe that our perception of the passing of time is related to our exposure to new and unique experiences.[6] In our younger years, everything is new and our lives are full of first-time experiences. Because of the way our brain processes and stores information, it seems that time passes more slowly. Over time, however, we're exposed to much less in the way of new experiences or new learning and everything becomes a blur of routine. We can slow the way we perceive the passing of time, believe scientists, if we embark on a journey of trying and learning new things and exposing ourselves to new situations.

Questions for Discussion and Introspection

Review your marketing materials and move-in paperwork. Listen to the way your team is talking about the community and what it has to offer. Is there a focus on elderhood as a time of continued growth? Or is the focus on who people were in the past? Are there opportunities for improvement in this area?

Where are conversations occurring that frame residents (and team members) as static beings, unable to learn a new approach or view of the world? How can the focus be shifted?

How do your current practices and policies encourage team member growth?

Who in your organization could begin driving a culture of growth? What next steps might you take to evaluate opportunities to drive this culture? What success stories of continued growth in your community can you share? Where are things going well in this aspect?

What story in this chapter resonated the most with you? Why?

CHAPTER 7

Give the Power (and Purpose) to the People

DURING OUR TRANSFORMATION at Clermont Park, we first began focusing on creating the culture of growth that we discussed in the last chapter. It was Dr. Roger Landry's keynote speech at a Clermont College of Creative Life graduation ceremony that got us thinking about moving beyond that focus to encouraging residents to find more ways to be of service to the community and to the world.

Too often, said Landry, we think of postretirement as "me time"—a time to indulge ourselves in what we want to do, or just do nothing and relax. While some self-indulgence is okay, he said, elders have much bigger and more important roles to play. Senior living communities, Landry suggested, are packed with human capital that has yet to be realized. AARP founder Ethel Percy Andrus offered this same observation decades ago when she launched an active retirement community, founded on the belief that "creative energy is ageless" and—in an era of forced retirement—it was society's loss to sideline its aging members. "Think of all the grand things we can do that youth can't," she extolled.

These insights from Landry and Andrus haven't become mainstream, however. Older people in retirement communities are often seen, as we learned in our discussion on community building in chapter 5, as helpless and passive recipients of services and care. And the resort-style hospitality approach often plays into and perpetuates this belief.

This view of senior living discounts older people and the role they can and should play in this world. We've made some progress in this area. Many communities have community service projects where residents knit hats for newborns or make toys for disadvantaged kids. One of my favorite initiatives at Clermont Park involved World War II residents teaching high school students about the war by sharing their personal perspectives and experiences.

These projects are fantastic. Finding more ways to share the knowledge, wisdom, and skills of older people provides critical opportunities for purpose. I believe we also have opportunities closer to home—encouraging resident engagement and influence in solving the problems within the senior living communities where they live.

We really don't expect much from residents. Instead, we focus much of our sales and marketing efforts on telling people what they will receive if they move to our community. Rarely do we ask the questions posed in chapter 5 (What will you bring to this community? How will you make it a better place?).

It's an interesting paradox. Our communities are full of knowledgeable, experienced individuals. Many are looking for purpose, but too often we view them as passive recipients of services and believe that the paid staff must do everything. Our communities and society lose out when we adopt this perspective.

By focusing on elders as people who still have purpose and meaning, we will do more than improve the culture in our communities. Meaningful purpose has been shown to reduce the risk of developing mild cognitive impairment and Alzheimer's disease,[1] increase longevity,[2] and protect against heart disease and stroke.[3] The stories in this chapter illustrate what happens when we recognize the power that elders have in holding meaningful and significant roles in our communities, and in the world.

What Happens in Vegas

One of my earliest lessons in empowerment came when I was the executive director of an assisted living community in Las Vegas.

It started with a report of a missing necklace.

We completed all of the necessary reporting, but I wasn't overly concerned. I assumed the item had been temporarily misplaced and would soon be found. A couple of days later, however, the resident was missing more jewelry and some cash. And a few days after that, I received another report, this time from a different resident. I knew then that this was more than misplaced items. We had serious theft going on. And it didn't stop. Every week I had more reports of missing items.

Each time, I would call the police. They dutifully responded but didn't offer much hope for identifying the thief. We had them attend staff meetings and our resident council meeting, asking everyone to be on the lookout for suspicious behavior.

Our resident council president, Bill, a big burley Marine with a strong protective instinct and a penchant for salty language, was incensed.

"We gotta find this sonofabitch!" he growled when he learned of the thefts. He then promptly dedicated himself to finding the culprit, patrolling the community in his electric scooter, which prominently displayed a bumper sticker for "The Few. The Proud. The Marines."

While Bill and the other residents and team members were on high alert, watching for suspicious activity, I started working on a secret sting operation to catch the thief. The interim director of maintenance, Jon, and I came up with a plan. We bought a hidden camera and invisible theft detection powder that would turn the culprits' hands a bright purple when he or she touched any item that the powder was sprinkled on. Since one resident, in particular, seemed to have a lot of theft activity occurring in her room, we got her permission to set up a sting operation in the living room of her apartment. We left powder-sprinkled money and jewelry in easy view.

We waited. But nothing happened. There were no purple hands. The jewelry and cash went untouched. But while the theft stopped in that apartment, it continued throughout the rest of the community. One morning, the daughter of a 100-year-old woman living with dementia reported that her mother's wedding and engagement rings, which had not been removed from her finger since she was married 80 years ago, were missing from her hand. We were devastated.

This time, when I made my police report, a new detective came to the building. He told me about a last-ditch effort that might work. He explained that every item sold in a pawn shop in the Las Vegas area is catalogued with the seller's information and stored in a database. He asked me to submit data on every employee of the community. I gave the list to the detective by the close of business that day.

A couple of days later, my phone rang. It was the detective.

"We have a match," he said.

It was Jon—the interim maintenance director. The guy I had trusted to help me with my sting operation. The person who was trusted and loved by residents, family members, and his colleagues. Jon and his wife had pawned thousands of dollars of merchandise over the prior months.

The detective sent me pages and pages of photos of rings, earrings, and necklaces that had been pawned by Jon and his wife. We started working on identifying the items so the police could issue a warrant for Jon's arrest.

Once an arrest warrant was issued, I called special resident and team member meetings to tell them about Jon. When I broke the news, everyone was devastated. Many were in tears.

Every single person in that community was victimized by Jon, whether he stole from them or not. The residents felt vulnerable and powerless.

Bill, in particular, was crushed. "I just feel so stupid," he said. "I trusted him. And he took advantage of all of us."

I was fortunate that my boss during this situation was a wise man named Dale Zulauf. He and I had many phone calls as the situation was unfolding. Part of me wanted to suppress the theft story and take care of the situation behind the scenes to avoid further stress on the residents, but as we talked, I understood that by taking that route I would be relegating the residents to a victim position. I realized I had a responsibility not only to protect the community, but also to support the residents in reclaiming their power and ensuring justice was done.

As we continued to identify additional pieces of pawned jewelry, the detective kept us informed of the new charges. He warned us that the Las Vegas district attorney's office had their hands full with "big" crimes and would likely let Jon plea bargain just to get the case through the courts. Jon could, he said, end up serving no jail time.

We could make a difference, the detective said, if we stayed on the DA's office and pressured them to reject a plea bargain. I talked with the residents and asked what they wanted to do. "Let's get that sonofabitch," said Bill. The others agreed. We worked together and called and wrote the DA's office regularly, demanding justice.

Finally, we were notified of Jon's sentencing date. The detective asked if I would make a statement at the sentencing. As had become our custom, I asked the residents how they wanted to proceed. "Yes! We'd like you to make a statement," they said, "but we're going with you."

On the day of Jon's sentencing, there was an air of excitement and purpose in the community. As we filled every seat on the community bus and headed for city hall, those who stayed behind at the building cheered us on from the door, wishing us luck and waving goodbye as we left.

It was quite a sight as we poured out of the bus and approached the security checkpoint at the courthouse.

"What's going on?" asked the guards, clearly puzzled by this influx of walkers and wheelchairs.

We filed into the courtroom and sat and waited. Then Jon and his attorney entered the courtroom. Bill, sitting next to me, growled. All of us glared at Jon. He looked away.

We listened to the proceedings and, when it was time, I made my statement asking for the maximum sentence. I introduced the residents and explained that I was speaking at their request and on behalf of the woman with the missing wedding rings, who, due to dementia, was unable to speak for herself. I explained how Jon must have pried the rings off her finger as she lay in her bed, powerless to stop him.

The judge sentenced Jon to no less than 5 years in a federal penitentiary. There was an outburst in the courtroom as the residents cheered and clapped. Our bus ride home was full of elation, high fives, and celebration. When we arrived back at the community, those who had stayed behind were waiting outside, cheering and clapping.

It was one of the most powerful and meaningful moments of my life. So often, older people are made to feel and believe that they're helpless victims. Rather than leaving a dark shadow over the community, the situation brought us together and made us all stronger—a perfect example of the power of the bonding that can occur during a difficult time, as discussed in chapter 5.

Ibasho

In 2011, a massive earthquake and typhoon struck northern Japan. More than 18,000 people were killed and another 65,000 were displaced. When disaster strikes, elders are usually viewed as helpless victims. In this situation, however, disaster survivors told stories of elders saving the lives of others by leading them to safety and teaching them how to survive with limited resources. The older people knew things that younger people didn't, such as where to run to when the waters rose and how to make rice without power and without a rice cooker.

Their wisdom saved lives.

Following the disaster, the elders of Ofunato, Japan, continued to play a critical role. Working with Emi Kiyota, an environmental gerontologist, they created the first Ibasho Café, an informal gathering place focused on driving recovery by providing valuable community services and support.

The café is a far cry from the traditional senior center where older adults are viewed as needy and passive recipients of services. *Ibasho* means "a place you can feel at home as yourself," and the Ibasho Café is run entirely by the elders of Ofunato. They drove the design of the project, oversee the structure and governance, and continue to make all of the day-to-day decisions.

The project was designed to empower elders to use their wisdom and experience to rebuild the devastated community. At the inception, says Kiyota, every person was asked what he or she could do to contribute. Some said they could wash dishes or cook, others offered to watch babies or make tea. Everyone found that they had a valuable skill or experience to share.

Kiyota's role was to provide tools and support and then leave and let the elders run the show. Five years after its inception, the Ofunato Ibasho Café is completely independent and self-sustaining, with elders even forgoing local government financial support so they can maintain their autonomy. They've continued to grow the organization, including cleaning up vacant lots to create a garden where they teach area children to plant and harvest vegetables and eat a healthy diet.

Kiyota founded Ibasho to reframe the identity of elders. The aging world population, she believes, will bankrupt us if we don't change our thinking and approach. It's economically impossible, she says, to provide care for the growing population of older people.

Ibasho reframes elders as valuable assets—people with life experience and knowledge that can help strengthen the resilience of the community—rather than as a population that just needs the rest of society to care for it. The philosophy is intended to teach and support elders in becoming part of the solution.

Because of the prevailing ageist mindset, however, Kiyota and Ibasho have had some push-back. Some people, for example, believed that Ibasho was putting too much pressure on elders. But Kiyota believes a certain level of stress is good. Too often we expect nothing of older people, and they come to believe they have nothing to give. Ibasho changes this perspective. The project has been replicated in Nepal and the Philippines. The Ofunoto elders provide peer-to-peer network support for both projects. In Nepal, the elder women fired the bricks that built the new building. There are great opportunities to adapt this mindset in other countries and areas where people are facing challenges and could benefit from the wisdom and experience of elders.

Keepers Committee

When Jayne Keller was the executive director of Holly Creek Life Plan Community, she struggled, as do many leaders, with retaining team members. One day she was reading through employee satisfaction surveys when it dawned on her that in almost every survey and every exit interview, team members gave the same response to the question about what they enjoy most about their job.

"Time after time," Keller recalls, "they said it was the residents that mattered the most to them."

She started thinking about how she could harness this information to improve retention and realized that residents could, and should, play a key role in solving the workforce dilemma.

Keller got a group of residents and team members together to talk about her idea. What came from that discussion is the Keepers Committee, a group of residents and nonsupervisory team members who meet each month to discuss new team members and any turnover that has occurred, and to share ideas about improving recruitment and retention.

The committee provides ongoing recognition to team members through personalized notes and celebrations. Committee members also mentor new associates to support them in their current and future jobs. The initiative has been very successful. Employee turnover has been reduced from 43 to 19 percent, quite an accomplishment in the Denver market, which is experiencing one of the lowest unemployment rates in the nation and an ever-escalating cost of living.

The work of the Keepers Committee expands beyond the actual committee members. The focus on the importance of retaining and supporting team members has spread throughout the community. Residents understand that they all play an important role in this initiative.

My parents live at this community, and I sometimes join them for dinner in Centennial's, the upscale dining venue. One evening, we had Rhianna, a brand new server, helping us. Rhianna was making a lot of mistakes. We had to wait an extended time for our meals, and in general things just weren't going well with our dinner experience.

I was getting frustrated with the poor service and was bracing myself for complaints from my parents. And then my mom said, "It's really hard to find and keep employees in this market. Rhianna is new here and it's our job to help her feel comfortable and be successful in her job." She then went on to compliment Rhianna on her efforts, praised her for doing such a great job on her first night, and told her to hang in there because it would get easier.

I almost fell out of my chair.

This was a clear departure from what I usually see in these settings, where residents get upset, grumble through dinner, and then fill out a comment card complaining about the service. I've visited communities where employees actually quit because residents treat them so badly when service is slow or mistakes are made.

The difference is that the residents at Holly Creek see themselves as more than consumers or customers. They see themselves as part of the solution. The Keepers Committee instilled a culture of support, kindness, and gratitude for team members. By understanding her role as a community leader, Keller didn't feel that she had to be the one with all the answers. She recognized that she had thousands of years of experience living right in her community. She didn't have to "own" the problem and shelter the residents from the struggles she was having. In a community, everyone owns problems and works through them together.

Ask Me!

I had the opportunity to harness the power of purpose with residents at Clermont Park during our extensive redevelopment project. Prior to the project, we were a quaint 40-year-old community with moderate-rate rental and HUD apartment homes, a nursing home, and an assisted living community.

Many had lived at the community for decades and were members of the church that had founded our organization. The building was modest and dated, but people were, for the most part, content. Their quiet world was soon to be upended, however, as construction equipment and workers moved on site. New spaces were being created. Multiple dining venues would take the place of the single traditional dining room. A fitness center, therapy gym, fellowship hall, and art studio were under construction.

Most intimidating of all, an influx of new residents would be coming into *their* home. These new residents, mostly people with higher income and asset levels, would be moving to life plan apartment homes and would be sharing common areas and resources with the existing resident population.

Our goal was to bring the community together as one of the few senior living communities in the country to integrate people of very different socioeconomic backgrounds. To some, it sounded impossible. There were fears that the community would end up much like New York City's mixed-use developments that were intended to integrate different populations but instead ended up continuing to segregate people, with lower income residents using what was termed a "poor door" to enter and exit the building.[4]

For me, the executive director at the time, this project was, indeed, a daunting challenge. I could already see the stress and angst bubbling up among the resident population. Even in the project's infancy, rumors were flying throughout the building, and residents were feeling extremely nervous.

At the time of the project, I had been learning about Nancy Fox, author and culture change expert, and The Eden Alternative's perspective on the role of a leader in times of change. During tumultuous times, Fox and The Eden Alternative teach that the leader's role is to calm the system and the chaos. My team and I knew that the best people to calm the system would be resident leaders. We couldn't do this without them.

We put out a call for assistance and invited anyone who was interested to attend an inaugural resident leadership meeting. We had a group of about a dozen participants. I explained, in detail, the upcoming project and my concerns—the stress and uncertainty that I was sensing in the community, and the worries about the existing resident population being ready to welcome a whole new group of neighbors.

We had many long discussions about the kind of culture we wanted to create. We talked about the importance of soothing the nerves of existing residents while warmly welcoming those who would be moving in. We discussed the role of resident leadership in calming the system and guiding the rest of the population to feel excitement rather than dread. I asked the group members if they would be willing to work with me on driving a cultural transformation.

They accepted the leadership challenge and got to work. The initiative went better than I ever expected.

The group's first step was to establish itself as a resource for the other residents. The group members bought large, bright red pins that said "Ask Me!" so all residents would know that they were the source of accurate information. The Ask Me! team's motto was, "If you don't hear it from us, it probably isn't true. If we don't have the answer, we'll find it for you." They went back out to their neighbors and peers to get a sense of the current climate. What were people worried about? What were they confused about? What information did they need?

Based on the feedback they received, we worked together to create a publication called "The Right Stuff." It included facts about the project and answers to commonly asked questions and worries. The publication went to all residents. A cover page listed the members of the Ask Me! team. Almost immediately, the angst and rumors float-ing throughout the community subsided.

The Ask Me! group learned that residents were nervous that, after construction, the community would be so large that getting to the new amenities would be difficult. We worked together to design signage to be placed on the interior construction barriers to provide information, such as, "When construction is done, the new Highline Restaurant will be only 20 steps from this location." This information immediately quashed the fears of reduced accessibility of the new spaces.

The enthusiasm of the Ask Me! group began to spread, and others realized they could play a role in strengthening the community. One day, a resident approached me, visibly upset. "I don't see how I can give back," she said. "I'm not a leader. I wasn't a teacher or a bigwig executive. What can I do?" We talked about her passions and skills, and she realized that her incredible baking skills could make a difference. She started baking for team members, which lifted their spirits during the difficult times of working in a construction zone. Others hosted a "Have a Cold One" drink booth for construction workers at the end of a long, hot day.

As the project moved forward, the Ask Me! group started focusing on approaches to eliminate the division that could easily occur between the existing and new residents. It was critical that we avoid a culture of "us" versus "them" and the "haves" versus the "have nots."

The Ask Me! group, through formal meetings and informal discus-sions, reminded other residents of how they felt when they first moved in and how unsettling it was not to know anyone. They spoke of their vision of an inclusive community where everyone would feel comfortable. They asked for assistance in welcoming the new residents and helping them to feel at home in the community. They talked about the importance of belonging.

It worked.

The community came together as one. It didn't matter who had a lot of money and who didn't, and who lived in a new apartment or an older one. If we had tried to drive this change from the community's formal leadership structure, it surely would have failed. It was powerful because it was created and driven by residents.

Dementia Action Alliance

People living with dementia are often the most stigmatized and dis-empowered of all. From the moment of diagnosis, many people living with dementia say the message they receive is one of hopelessness and helplessness. Because there's currently no medical treatment for the condition, they often hear upon diagnosis, "I'm so sorry. There's nothing we can do. I suggest you go home and get your affairs in order." What's missing in this well-intended approach is hope for living a meaningful life with a diagnosis of dementia.

Dementia Action Alliance (DAA) is an organization working to shift that mindset. Those involved with DAA are professionals, care partners, and, most importantly, individuals living with dementia. The organization seeks to eliminate the stigma of dementia and create opportunities for continued growth, purpose, and joy.

Nothing is done, no decisions are made, without those living with dementia being involved and their voices being heard.

I was first introduced to DAA at a LeadingAge PEAK leadership summit when I attended a session about dementia. Now, I've been to many dementia education sessions over the years, but this was the first time I was taught by the *true* experts—those who are living with the condition.

The panelists spoke of their personal experiences in being diagnosed and living with dementia, and the need to fight the overwhelming and debilitating stigma that is so often experienced. Stigma burdens them with unnecessary challenges that impede their ability to be proactive and resilient with a degenerative, chronic condition. An early diagnosis provides the opportunity to connect with others living with dementia, plan for the future, and develop a supportive network.

One of the widespread myths is that people living with dementia can't learn new skills. The panelists disputed this claim, citing technology and other adaptive approaches that empower them to retain independence and live full lives.

Many of these panelists, who refer to themselves as dementia advocates, travel the country, and some, the world, educating and mentoring people and providing a much-needed message of hope through engagement, empowerment, and community inclusion.

I've had the great fortune to get to know some of these inspiring folks, including Brian LeBlanc.

LeBlanc, whose tag line is, "I have Alzheimer's, but it doesn't have me!," is a gregarious and inspirational activist, keynote speaker, writer, and team member for Dementia Friendly Cruises. While he admits he has down days and tough times, LeBlanc says his dementia diagnosis has enriched his life and taught him how to live.

"I'm having a blast," he told me the last time I saw him. "I've found my purpose."

Sometimes It's the Little Things

When working toward creating a culture of empowerment, we often want to look for the big events—the "wow" moments, like elders finding purpose in a disaster or creating a new community culture or dementia advocacy organization. But sometimes it's the little things that tell the best story. One day, Brad Boatright, community executive director, and I were walking through the nursing home at Casey's Pond Senior Living. As we walked through the building, we came upon a common area space. There sat a group of six residents. They had a huge crossword puzzle spread out on an ottoman between them. One of the residents was reading clues to the others. They were all thoroughly engaged and laughing. Boatright and I stopped to chat for awhile. One of the residents introduced herself and said that she was the person responsible for the resident store. Her face was beaming. We joked around for a bit and tried to come up with the word for the clue they were working on.

As we walked away, I realized how rare this was to see in a nursing home. There wasn't a staff member there. And "crossword puzzle time" wasn't on the activity calendar. This was just a group of residents who decided they wanted to do something together. The community made sure they had supplies, a space to do what they wanted to do, and the empowerment to do it.

So often, we see people, especially in nursing homes, who are so institutionalized and dependent that they think they can't do anything unless it's scheduled on a calendar and run by team members. Real life doesn't work that way.

As The Eden Alternative teaches us, life happens between the big scheduled programs. How often in our lives outside of work do we participate in scheduled events every day from morning until night? During the holiday season, when many people have event after event and little downtime, we wind up exhausted. We long for unscheduled, unscripted time—for the spontaneity to do what we want to do. To read. Or nap. Or do nothing at all, if we wish.

Why then are regulatory compliance and organizational success based on staff-driven activity calendars packed with back-to-back group activities from morning to night? I believe that much of the exhaustion and blank looks that we see in nursing homes are people who've just checked out because they've had enough—enough of being pushed in their wheelchairs from planned event to planned event all day long and sitting in a chair in an activity room watching entertainers play music that they're not interested in.

What if we stopped focusing on filling up the squares on a calendar and instead focused on empowering people by providing the equipment, supplies, and space (both literal and figurative) to do what they want to do?

Questions for Discussion and Introspection

Pay attention to what you see, read, and hear on the news. Where are elders positioned as victims versus as part of the solution? How can you begin to change the conversation?

What are some examples of meaningful purpose in your community? How can you share and celebrate those stories?

Where are there opportunities in your organization for elders to play a meaningful role, to share their wisdom and skills to make the community stronger and more resilient?

What story in this chapter resonated the most with you? Why?

How might you go about taking next steps to create more opportunities for purpose?

CHAPTER 8

It's My Life

Paternalism and Surplus Safety

My GRANDMOTHER WAS a proud, no-nonsense woman with a dry sense of humor. She and my grandfather owned and ran a small grocery store in a little town in upstate New York. They lived in a 900-square-foot apartment above that store for more than 50 years. After they retired and closed the store, my grandparents enjoyed a couple of years of fun and travel. Then my grandfather's health started to fail. He was diagnosed with leukemia. And then he developed circulatory issues in both of his legs, which eventually resulted in a double amputation. Since their apartment was accessible only by climbing a long and narrow flight of stairs from the street entrance next to their storefront, they had a chair lift installed. Still, getting out was extremely difficult. My grandfather, and to some extent my grandmother, was essentially trapped in the home for many years.

I don't remember either of them losing their sense of humor or positive outlook, but I'm sure some days were really rough. When my grandfather passed away, my grandmother, at age 80, did some interesting things. When people would ask if she wanted to remarry, she'd reply, "Hell no! I was happy to take care of my husband, but I'm not taking care of another man."

This was clearly her time to live. At a point in life when most people would downsize, my grandmother went in search of a large house with a yard and a garden, something she had never been able to have in her adult life. She found a huge, four-bedroom, two-story house with a basement and a big yard and immediately went to work hiring contractors to make it the home she had always wanted.

When I saw her new place for the first time, I was beside myself.

Here she was, 80 years old and living alone in a big house with a long, steep staircase she had to climb to get to her bedroom. And the basement staircase was even worse! It was a creaky, wooden apparatus that was so steep I had to hold the handrail to safely descend. It was terrifying. There was so much space—and there were so many dangers. I knew too well all the ways that my grandmother could get hurt.

"Grandma!" I exclaimed, "This scares me. You know there are great senior living communities where you could live. They have elevators and lots of things to do, and people to help you if you ever need help."

"Yes, I know," she'd say, interrupting my sales pitch, "but that's not for me."

And she was right. While I knew better than anyone the benefits of community living, it wouldn't have been a fit for my grandmother. She truly enjoyed being alone and puttering around her house. I don't think she ever felt lonely or isolated. She went to the senior center regularly. Not as a participant (God forbid! My grandmother, like most of us, had her own internalized ageist beliefs), but as a volunteer to help the "old people." She had a full life.

"Well," I countered, "since you won't consider moving, will you promise not to go down in the basement by yourself?"

"Nope," she replied, making it clear that there was no opportunity for negotiation.

"Well, then will you at least get one of those 'I've fallen and I can't get up' pendants?" I begged.

Again, she refused. "I have a cordless phone, I'll carry that with me."

And she stuck with that, living in that big old house for 12 years. Eventually she did get an emergency call pendant, but she was steadfast in her refusal to consider moving into a retirement community or to even move closer to my parents, who lived 3 hours away. She made it clear that she needed to continue to be in control of her own life—and that sometimes meant making decisions we didn't agree with. We had to learn to be okay with that.

Over time, she started having episodes where she'd end up in the emergency room. My parents noticed when they went to visit that she had outdated food in her refrigerator, and her house wasn't quite as clean as it used to be. We knew things were changing. But still, she wouldn't move.

We always spent Christmas with my grandmother at my parent's house. During one holiday visit, my grandmother, then 92, seemed a little "off" and a tad more forgetful. We were worried, but she insisted on going back home after the holiday. My dad took her home the day after Christmas. Two days later, she died. From what we can surmise, she had a heart attack in the middle of the night. There was evidence that she may have suffered a bit and spent some time walking around her house, confused, before she died. But she lived her life the way she wished. I know if I could ask her, she would say she had no regrets about the choices she made. Or the way she had died.

It had taken me, and my family, a very long time to get to a place of acceptance, where we could truly honor and respect the decisions she was making. Like so many families, we just wanted to keep our grandmother safe. I'm thankful that she was as tough as she was. Had we forced or cajoled her into moving, she very well may have lived longer, but it would have been at the expense of making her own choices and decisions—something that was essential to her well-being.

I've seen too many times the way that paternalism, defined as behavior that limits a person's liberty or autonomy for what is presumed to be that person's own good, drives our decisions in senior living settings.

Undermining Autonomy

John Ahlenius is well known at Clermont Park. He's an artist, a performer, a cyclist, and an outspoken advocate for social justice. He teaches drumming exercise classes (yes, there is such a thing!) and is always one to question the status quo. A bachelor, Ahlenius lives in an apartment home that he colorfully describes as "a man cave with undertones of urban grit." His cave features treasures from his travel around the world and a large metal wall sculpture that Ahlenius created. On his patio sits his private hot tub. Beyond that, his convertible sports car and motor scooter gleam in the parking lot.

Everything about Ahlenius' apartment home screams, "I march to the beat of my own drum."

Before moving to the community, he had lived in a contemporary loft a short distance from Coors Field baseball stadium in downtown Denver, where he often volunteers. Ahlenius was intrigued by the new apartment homes geared toward active adults being built at our community. He agreed to move in as long as our walls could accommodate his huge sculptures and as long as our electrical system could accommodate a dedicated line for his patio hot tub. I was happy to accommodate both requests.

But then things got a little tricky. Soon after Ahlenius moved in, he visited me one day to discuss adding a gate from his patio to the parking lot. He wanted to easily get to his car without walking through the building to an exit door.

"We can't do that," I told him, explaining that the exterior of the patios needed to be consistent from apartment to apartment.

"Fine." he said, "Then let me put a step on the outside of my patio wall so I can hop over."

"Oh, geez, I'm sorry," I replied, with a worried look on my face, "That wouldn't be safe. You could fall and get hurt if you jumped over the wall."

Used to living a life doing as he pleased, Ahlenius was not happy. He left my office very upset and returned multiple times, pleading his case. I talked with our risk management team, and they agreed that a step would be dangerous. So I held firm.

Eventually, his patience wore thin. He stormed into my office one day and proclaimed, "Look, I'm going to jump over the wall either way, so adding a step would at least minimize my risk of falling. And really, shouldn't I be the one making decisions about whether I'm okay with the risk? I've been making decisions my whole life."

Ahlenius went on to explain that his children were constantly worried about him riding his scooter. They were afraid he would have an accident and get hurt. "I tell them to take that worry off of themselves," he said, "I remind them that this is *my* decision. I'm not hurting anyone else, and if I die riding my scooter, they should know that I died doing what I love. It's the same thing with this step. It's my life, not yours, and the risk is worth it to me."

It finally sunk in. Ahlenius was right. Like my grandmother, he *should* be the one deciding what risks he wanted to take. I had been so worried about him getting hurt and our organization being sued that I had created a stifling environment. We were trying to keep him safe from a fall but were squashing the spirit of a nonconformist guy—a guy who needed freedom to be happy. My approach was a clear contradiction of the life of independence and freedom we were selling to the residents.

I went back to our risk management team. After sharing Ahlenius' reasoning and having a thorough discussion, we decided that the benefits of supporting him in making his own decisions far outweighed the risk to the organization. Ahlenius put in a step, and he hops over it to this day.

I'm embarrassed when I think about my initial response to John's request. And I'm even more ashamed of my behavior many years before with a nursing home resident, and retired attorney, who I'll call Fred. Fred lived in the nursing home I managed. His son, who was very involved, lived nearby and visited often.

It wasn't long after I started my job that a nurse found a bottle of aspirin in Fred's room and brought it to my office. Fred had some pretty complex medications that needed nurse oversight, and, because of that, the nursing team had determined that he couldn't self-administer anything.

I went to Fred's room, bottle of pills in hand, and told him we'd have to lock the bottle in the medication cart, get a physician order, and have the nurses administer the pills. Fred's face hardened. He demanded to keep the aspirin in his room. He argued that he was of sound mind and should be able to take aspirin whenever he wanted to. I stood my ground and took the bottle of aspirin away.

Then Fred's son came to see me.

"Please," he begged, "this is the only control my dad has left in his life. He was a powerful lawyer who was in charge of everything. All of that is gone. He just needs to have control over *something*. Please let him do this."

Again, I refused. I explained that while I respected his dad's wishes, we couldn't take on the liability for his dad keeping that aspirin in his room.

It turned into an all-out war with Fred. And it went on for months. Fred would come to my office and swear at me. He would threaten me and swing his walker at me. His son stopped by repeatedly and begged me to reconsider. And still, I held firm. I was, after all, the administrator who was responsible for his safety. I had policies and regulations to follow.

Eventually, Fred gave up. He stopped coming to my office. He stopped swinging his walker at me and threatening me. Instead, he sat in his room staring at the wall. He followed the rules. He became compliant.

To this day, it hurts deeply to know that I was *that* administrator, who was so hung up on my interpretation of the regulations and so afraid of risk that, rather than investigating options and creative solutions with Fred (of which I now know there were many!), I took away the one small thing that would have given him some control and freedom. Rather than being a good part of the last years of his life, Fred's time at my community left him feeling frustrated and defeated.

It's disturbing that I had the power to make decisions for John and Fred, and other residents who were well over twice my age and with twice the life experience. Yet that is the culture of senior living and of healthcare. We assume that just because someone is older and needs some assistance, the person can no longer make decisions about risk or how he or she wishes to live his or her life.

I wasn't a bad person. And I wasn't trying to hurt John or Fred. I just didn't know of any other way.

In retrospect, I think I was overwhelmed by the risk, liability, and responsibility of being an administrator. With constant reminders of all the ways I could get into hot water with lawyers and regulators, I was acting from a place of fear rather than common sense. Judging from posts on a Facebook group of nursing home administrators that I'm a member of, I don't think I'm alone in that all-consuming focus. The vast majority of posts are related to concerns about risk management and regulatory compliance, with several posts asking for "thoughts and prayers" for communities in the midst of their annual state health department survey (inspection).

Surplus Safety

A few years ago, the organization I worked for assumed management of a community that boasted a gorgeous outdoor living area. It had amazing views of the mountains, comfortable seating, and a gas fire pit. I was so excited. I imagined all the fun things that could happen around that pit—gatherings with grandchildren and campfire stories and s'mores. I asked the community leadership team how they used the space.

"We haven't used that pit since the building opened," they said. "We're afraid someone will get burned." No one thought a thing of it. No one pushed back or questioned this decision. But when this focus on safety happens in other environments, the response can be a bit different. In 2013, a school in Port Washington, New York, concerned about student safety, banned baseballs and footballs on the playground and required that tag and cartwheels be supervised by a coach.[1] During that same year, the U.S. Postal Service pulled the plug on postage stamps inspired by First Lady Michelle Obama's Let's Move! campaign because they portrayed characters engaged in what were considered to be unsafe activities, such as cannonball dives into swimming pools and kids doing handstands without wearing helmets.[2]

These stories sparked scorn and outrage in the media and the public, resulting in colorful commentary about the inherent necessity of scrapes and bruises as a part of growing up, and questions as to the future of a society that has such a suffocating focus on safety. Cheryl K. Chumley, in her editorial headline for the *Washington Times*, referred to the ball ban as a "sign of the apocalypse."[3] And, in an op-ed piece, former Connecticut governor John Rowland stated, "There are countless stories like this across the country and I am all for protecting our kids, but let them play, let them scrape their knees, maybe even twist an ankle, it's all part of growing up."[4]

In contrast, there is little to no outrage about the bland and stifling environments that we create in nursing homes and retirement communities in the name of risk management. A mother who wouldn't allow her child to sit by a campfire toasting marshmallows would be called a helicopter parent. Yet no one blinked an eye when a retirement community stripped that right away from people who had lived for many decades and could make their own decisions.

Many things we think are fun involve some level of risk. Skiing, playing sports, and traveling all come with the risk of injury—or worse. Even the most mundane activities of daily life can be fraught with danger. The simple steps of getting out of bed, walking down the stairs, and driving to work involve risk, yet we do take these steps every day. As Dr. Bill Thomas says, "The only completely risk-free human environment is a coffin."[5] Most people would agree that a life without risk is not a life worth living.

Why, then, do we think all risk must end when we reach a certain age?

Just as I saw every potential danger in my grandmother's new house, we in the field of aging services are highly skilled in the art of identifying every bad thing that can happen. Mistakes in our world, after all, are often met with harsh punishments from the department of health and the legal system. As a result, we've become experts at quickly assessing a situation and immediately spotting every trip hazard, every error, every potential mistake that could get us sued, tagged during a state or federal inspection, or in hot water with our corporate office. Wanting to keep everyone safe, we bubble wrap our organizations with policies and procedures and rules and end up suffocating everyone in the process.

Drs. Bill Thomas and Judah Ronch call this negative approach to risk assessment "surplus safety"—the tendency to look only at the downside or negative risk of a situation.[6] In reality, though, risk is multidimensional. There is indeed downside risk (the chance that things will turn out worse than we expect), but there is also upside risk (the chance that things will turn out better than we expect).

Thomas and Ronch propose that we use a more balanced approach, one in which potential upside risk is evaluated as we make decisions. So, for example, in evaluating the fire pit scenario, we would have to work past our initial fear-driven reaction of people getting burned and look at the good things that could come from people sitting around a campfire. Residents and team members could bond and people could sing songs, tell ghost stories, and have fun! Those opportunities for positive experiences have to play into our evaluations.

A Balanced Approach

This type of thinking—of evaluating all sides of a situation—requires discipline. I was fortunate to work with Russ DenBraber, former president and CEO of Christian Living Communities, who was a master at finding this balance. We'd be in risk management meetings discussing an incident, and, without fail, someone would start going down the surplus safety road of evaluating only the downside risk. DenBraber would remind us that it's the job of our insurance companies and lawyers to help us identify risk, but it's up to organizational leaders to ensure that risk is balanced with community and quality of life. It's called risk *management*, he would say, not risk elimination.

An organizational culture of surplus safety often leads to suffocating oversight of residents (my reactions to John and Fred are perfect examples). And nowhere is this culture more prevalent than in nursing homes, where surplus safety intertwines tightly with paternalism.

It's evident in the things we say and the way we document situations in nursing notes. Phrases such as "she's noncompliant" and "he's refusing his medications" are scattered liberally throughout daily conversations and nursing notes. In saying and writing these things, we diminish the abilities and experiences of elders and their right to make decisions. And we rarely question any of it.

When I'm doing training, I take participants through an exercise in which I ask them all to stand up. I tell them I'm going to ask them a series of questions and they should sit down when they can answer "yes" to any of them. I then ask them the following:

- Do you smoke?

- Do you sleep less than 7 to 8 hours per night?

- Do you drink sugary or diet sodas?

- Do you eat candy and processed foods?

- Do you drink more than the recommended amount of alcohol?

- Do you eat fatty foods?

- Do you drink more than two cups of coffee a day?

One by one, everyone ends up answering "yes" and sitting down.

"Aha!" I say to them. "You are all noncompliant with what a doctor says you should do."

Then I ask them how they react when someone tells them to start doing healthier things. "I tell them to butt out," they say. "It's my life."

Older adults have this same right, no matter where they are living, and no matter what type of help they need. Simply moving into a nursing home or assisted living community shouldn't change that. We must change our thinking and use words that illustrate an older person's right to continue making choices, even if we disagree with them, and even if they are bad decisions in the opinion of medical experts.

No matter what our age, we have what Thomas calls "the right to folly" or the right to make our own decisions, even if they're bad decisions, as long as we're not hurting other people.

Author and culture change expert Nancy Fox reminds us that, while we often cite regulations as the basis for our surplus safety decisions, CMS (Centers for Medicare and Medicaid Services) regulations guarantee that nursing home residents have all the same rights as any other U.S. citizen. Chief among those rights, Fox says, are the inalienable rights of life, liberty, and the pursuit of happiness.

The words we use to describe people acting on these rights have a significant impact on our thoughts and behaviors and the way we view elders living in our communities.

Imagine being a nurse who is coming in to work. You pull up the prior shift's nurses notes and read that new resident Mrs. Smith "refused her shower" and was "noncompliant with therapy orders." "Ugh," you'd say to yourself, "this Mrs. Smith is going to be a problem. She sounds like a troublemaker." And that belief would color every interaction you have with Mrs. Smith and your interpretation of everything that she says and does. Imagine instead reading that Mrs. Smith *chose* to sleep in instead of taking a shower and that she *decided* she wasn't interested in therapy today because her daughter was coming to visit. Those alternative phrases take away the judgment and the paternalistic views of older people. They support Mrs. Smith being who she is and living life as she chooses.

When I'm doing consulting work, I often recommend as a first step that teams eliminate the words *refuse* and *noncompliant* from their vocabulary and instead speak and document using words that reflect a resident making choices. Without fail, this small change has a significant impact on the way team members view residents.

Surplus Safety Audits

After my experience with John and his patio step, I took a long hard look at myself and the culture we were creating at my community. We started focusing on identifying and eliminating surplus safety and paternalism. Instead of conducting the very common safety audit, we took the opposite approach and conducted a surplus safety audit. The goal was to shine a light on unnecessary, paternalistic, and cumbersome rules and practices. I started this work with a group of residents who lived in our independent living neighborhood (where, in theory, there should be less paternalism and surplus safety) and asked them to look at every rule, every policy, every document they had received as a resident. What they brought back to me was both fascinating and troubling.

The first policy to come under scrutiny was a long-standing rule that a resident could not push another person in a wheelchair. Residents had long thought it was ludicrous and that it took away the opportunity to be a good friend and a neighbor. Yet the prior administration had stuck to that rule. When we dug into the history behind the policy, we learned that, years ago, someone had been injured when being pushed in a wheelchair by another resident. One situation. And a new policy had been enacted that took away the opportunity for purpose and friendships and community. When we looked at the upside of people pushing each other in wheelchairs, we realized that the benefits of community, of purpose, and of being a good friend to another outweighed the small risk of someone getting hurt.

Another rule stated that residents couldn't use their dining spend-down accounts to purchase meals for a friend or neighbor. When we researched the history of the policy, the underlying reasoning was paternalism. What if someone was taken advantage of by another resident?

What if the resident then cut herself short on meals for the month because of the decision? This type of thinking quickly institutionalizes people and exacerbates the belief that older people can't make decisions for themselves. Will some people take advantage of others and act only in their best interest? Probably, but that is the exception, not the rule. We can't make decisions and policies and rules based on the bad behavior of the 1 percent or the rare accident that occurs.

One day, during this surplus safety audit process, my patio wall-hopping friend John Ahlenius burst into my office with the resident handbook. "Look at this!" he exclaimed, jabbing his finger at a page of the handbook. "This says we can't have birdfeeders because it could attract squirrels or mice."

"What?" I asked. "That's ridiculous, let me see that." And sure enough, there, in the updated version of the handbook that I myself had reviewed and approved, was that stupid rule.

Once we got past our fear of risk and I started to get over the need to control everything, our community focused on supporting people in making their own decisions about risk. Residents wanted to play ping-pong on the weekends, so every Saturday morning our maintenance team would set up the ping-pong table in the fitness center. Residents and team members had a blast. One weekend, a resident tripped and fell while playing and ended up in the emergency room. When I saw the incident report, I'll admit that small fearful voice in my head returned, saying, "We need to get rid of the ping-pong table." But fortunately, common sense prevailed. The resident herself said: "Things happen! Sometimes people fall when they're having fun. It's part of life."

Another resident was a master gardener. When she moved into our community, she said she'd like to take care of all of the rose bushes on campus. She did a beautiful job. The roses flourished, as did she. One day, as she was reaching to prune a bush, she tripped and fell and broke her hip. Even as she lay in her nursing home bed after surgery, she said she would be getting right back to her gardening work as soon as she was able. She wasn't willing to give up her love of gardening and her role in the community even though she knew she could fall and get hurt again.

Nothing Grows in a Culture of Fear

These examples are positively elementary compared to the work being done by Angie McAllister and her organization, Signature HealthCARE. McAllister has long been someone who pushes the envelope. When she worked at a Signature community as quality of life director, she had nursing home residents in helicopters and on jet skis. Now Director of Quality of Life and Culture Change, McAllister leads and guides cultural transformation at 115 Signature communities. If you follow Signature HealthCARE on Facebook (and I recommend that you do!), you won't see the usual photos of residents sitting in chairs being passively entertained. Instead, you might see postings of elders swimming with dolphins, sightseeing in cities, or hanging out at the beach.

These elder vacations started in 2011 when a resident mentioned to the community's quality of life director that he wanted to go to Disney World. After the resident agreed that he was okay having others join him on a trip, the team member went to her nursing team and asked, "Can we make this happen?" Because of the organization's culture, the nurses didn't respond by pointing out every reason that it couldn't work. They figured it out and problem-solved. Twenty four elders went on that inaugural trip, and since then around 700 skilled nursing residents have taken part in a Signature vacation. They've gone to myriad destinations, including New York City, San Antonio, and Myrtle Beach, to name a few.

The trips have had an incredible impact on the vacationers. The *Lexington Herald-Leader* shared the story of James, who had been a logger and worked in the tobacco fields his whole life. He'd never had the time or money to visit the beach and felt that his lack of education would impede him in trying to get there on his own. Yet he'd always dreamed of seeing the ocean. As a resident of a Signature HealthCARE home, James was finally able to realize that dream during a trip to Myrtle Beach. As he told the newspaper reporter, "If I die, I'd be satisfied."[7]

McAllister has spoken about the trips at conferences and has been interviewed in industry publications. Everyone who hears about these trips thinks it's an amazing idea. Yet, to her knowledge, few communities have tried it. The reason, she says, is probably fear.

McAllister understands the fear and worry that come with supporting residents when they engage in life outside of a nursing home. A turning point in her career came before the elder vacations. A resident fell and got hurt during an outing to a bowling alley. McAllister was terribly upset, wondering what she could have done to prevent the fall. Maybe if the resident hadn't been bowling, she thought, he wouldn't have sustained the injury. But when she went with the resident for medical treatment, the doctor said something she'll always remember.

"He could have fallen and gotten hurt at the nursing home in the normal course of the day," the doctor said. Instead, "he got hurt having fun and doing what he wanted to do. How can that be a bad thing?"

The cure for fear, says McAllister, "is to lean into it." When they first considered these vacations, her biggest worry was violating regulatory requirements. So she called the department of health and shared the idea. The regulators thought elder vacations was a fantastic idea and helped her organization to work through the details of pulling off such a feat while maintaining regulatory compliance.

"Nothing grows in a culture of fear," says McAllister, "and some bad things will happen."

Have they had residents end up in the emergency room during these trips? Yep. People have fallen, sustained injuries, and gotten sick on vacation. But in their minds, that isn't a reason to stop. According to McAllister, in the Signature culture of balanced risk assessment, the joy, the good things, and the novel experiences outweigh the downside risk.

Because no chapter about risk would be complete without a disclaimer, I want to leave you with a few more points. First, I am not an attorney, a regulator, or an insurance professional. It's wise to always consult with those experts and have an open dialogue with them about how you can evaluate both upside and downside risk, with the goal being to mitigate risk while maintaining a culture where life is worth living. Changing an organization's risk culture is a really big deal and shouldn't be taken lightly. It requires a great deal of conversation with both internal and external stakeholders. I recommend lots of discussion and then starting with small, fairly innocuous situations. As your team becomes more comfortable with full evaluation of upside and downside risk, that's the time to move on to riskier territory.

Questions for Discussion and Introspection

What is your current risk management process? What is the balance of evaluation of upside and downside risk?

How can you work with your organization to develop a more balanced approach to risk evaluation?

Conduct a surplus safety audit, and include elders and team members. Where does surplus safety exist in your organization? Why do you think this is?

How do current policies and procedures undermine autonomy?

Which story in this chapter resonated the most with you? Why?

What might be a next step to take to begin to evaluate risk in a different way? Who needs to be involved in these exploratory discussions?

CHAPTER 9

Making It Happen

Lessons in Change Leadership

YEARS AGO, when I started working to change the culture in nursing homes, I was unprepared for just how difficult the transformation would be. I was the administrator of a very large institutional nursing home. At the urging of the ombudsman, I attended a Certified Eden Associate Training. It set me on fire!

Finally, I had the tools I needed and the understanding that things really could be different.

I immediately started taking steps to eliminate the institutional model. But no matter how hard I worked, things weren't changing fast enough for me. It seemed like we were moving at a snail's pace. We would take one step forward and two, or sometimes three, steps back. I bumped up against more obstacles than I ever imagined, including team members who were reluctant to get on board.

One day, I was talking with my organization's CEO about the process and my frustration with the pace of transformation. He told me something I'll never forget. He said that organizations are like big old wooden ships. When you turn the wheel of a big ship, he explained, it's not like steering a car. The vessel doesn't immediately change course. It takes time. The ship will groan and creak as it turns, fighting the wind and the waves. It's slow going, he said, but eventually, it *will* shift and move in the direction you want to go. And that's exactly what happened.

I want to save other leaders from that initial frustration and despair that I felt. If we understand that the creaking and groaning and slow-moving change are normal, we're much more likely to keep going when things get tough.

The cold hard fact is that an estimated 70 percent of change efforts fail.[1] For the 30 percent of efforts that are successful, the path is full of obstacles, mistakes, and problems. And, like any cultural transformation, the work is never done. Once you think you have it figured out, you realize there's more work to be done and more growing to do. I share this not to scare you or make you give up, but to help prepare you for the journey.

This chapter isn't intended to be an all-inclusive toolbox of transformation tools—there are plenty of excellent books and change leadership resources out there. Rather, it's a compilation of some of the most helpful shifts in thinking that I've picked up from other people along the way and through my experiences with the LeadingAge Leadership Academy and The Eden Alternative. They're the things I wish I'd known when I first started doing organizational transformation work.

Expect Opposition

One of the most frustrating and exhausting parts of change leadership is trying to get people on board. We'll spend a lot of time in this chapter exploring resistance and how to work around it and overcome it. But the first, most important lesson of all is to expect it.

People *will* push back.

They'll say it's impossible. They won't want to change. Don't let that get you down. As Albert Einstein said, "If at first an idea is not absurd, then there is no hope for it."

In his book, *Originals: How Nonconformists Move the World,* Adam Grant explains that "in the face of uncertainty, our first instinct is to reject novelty and look for reasons that the unfamiliar concepts will fail."[2] Many of the things we now take for granted were once ridiculed when they were first introduced—umbrellas, personal computers, lightbulbs, just to name a few, were rejected. Even handwashing, which we now know to be the most basic and important step we can take in infection control, was once rejected and ridiculed. Grant tells the story of the doctor who first introduced handwashing as a means of reducing death rates during childbirth. Rather than being celebrated, this doctor was scorned by his colleagues. It took 20 years for his theory to be legitimized in the medical field!

In the field of aging services, think about restraints and side rails. They were once the norm in nursing homes and there were many naysayers when the push was made for their elimination. Keep examples such as these in your mind, and when you encounter opposition, celebrate it—it means you're doing something different!

Adaptive versus Technical Challenges

One of the many transformational experiences of the LeadingAge Leadership Academy is being immersed in the study of adaptive leadership, a theory developed and pioneered by Ronald Heifetz.[3] It was like a lightbulb going off when I learned this theory because it explained a lot of the challenges and failures I had experienced when trying to implement change.

Adaptive leadership is much different than the type of work we're used to doing in our field. We're well-trained to identify and respond to what Heifetz calls "technical challenges." Technical challenges are ones that are easy to identify and diagnose, can usually be fixed by an expert, and require small changes in just one or two areas. Because technical fixes are generally fast and painless, people are usually very responsive to technical solutions.

In contrast, the type of transformational work we've been discussing in this book is what Heifetz would call an adaptive challenge. Adaptive challenges are much harder to identify than technical challenges. We likely know there's a problem, but we don't really know what it is. Adaptive challenges can't be solved by an expert or through the implementation of quick fixes. Rather, they require the people who are experiencing the problem to fix the problem. People have to change the way they think, what they believe, and the way they work together. And change usually needs to happen throughout an entire organization or system. Finally, solutions come only through trial and experimentation—and usually lots of mistakes. Adaptive work takes time and patience. People usually resist adaptive challenges and adaptive work.

A perfect example of technical versus adaptive solutions is the approach most people take when they receive a new medical diagnosis. A few years ago, my otherwise healthy 40-something husband, Todd, suddenly began having excruciating pain when he got out of bed in the morning. He went to the doctor and, after myriad tests, was diagnosed with rheumatoid arthritis, a painful inflammatory disease.

Todd's rheumatologist talked with him about options for treatment. There were technical solutions, such as medications and injections, and adaptive solutions, which would require that Todd change his sleep, stress management, eating, and exercise habits. With lifestyle changes, the doctor told him, he probably wouldn't need pills or shots.

Guess which option Todd chose? Yep! He went for the technical fix, getting medication and injections and changing little about his lifestyle. Todd, like most of us, was drawn to the technical solution because it was easier.

That same proclivity to seek the easy-to-identify solution occurs in our work in senior living. As gerontologist Sonya Barsness says, we gravitate toward quick and easy-to-define fixes, things we can list on banners or on our websites. But technical fixes applied to adaptive challenges are rarely effective. John Cochrane, president and CEO of HumanGood agrees. "When we look at attracting a new generation of older adults," says Cochrane, "we're drawn to quick fixes, like switching out linoleum for granite, and don't realize that the real change that needs to happen is much deeper."

In my work with The Eden Alternative, I've come across many such examples. When I first wanted to introduce the Ten Principles of The Eden Alternative to that big old nursing home, my team responded with pessimism. "It won't work," they said. "Our last administrator tried it." What the last administrator had done, however, was to pick up on one tiny piece of The Eden Alternative philosophy—introducing pets into a community.

The team hadn't done any foundational adaptive work or shifted their way of thinking and doing things in the organization. Instead, the administrator went out and got some kittens and brought them to live at the community. As you can imagine, it was a complete disaster. The kittens climbed the curtains, scratched residents, and created havoc. The experiment didn't last long.

In another organization, we were concerned that many residents were lonely. To solve the problem, we implemented a corporate initiative called the "guardian angel program," whereby each team member was assigned to a resident to be his or her friend. In my community, we went so far as to create spreadsheets to document the visits.

We limped along with the program, never really getting any traction. About a year later, as we had moved ahead in our culture change journey, I was sitting in a meeting with my team discussing the initiatives that had been on our radar in the past. The guardian angel program came up and one of my team members said, "The guardian angel program is the most institutional approach I've ever seen used to try to fix the institutional model."

She was right.

We were faced with an adaptive challenge and had attempted to use a technical solution to fix it. The effective, adaptive solution required a complete shift in our thinking and in the way we did things. We had to change our whole culture and mindset from one of task provision to meaningful relationships. Once we did that deep and meaningful adaptive work, we didn't need a guardian angel program. Relationships developed organically.

Other organizations attempt to eliminate the institutional model of care by building a new building or by eradicating scrubs or medication carts, but do so without any of the deep transformation that needs to occur. As with the kitten fiasco or the guardian angel program, these efforts usually fail. The real work of culture change is a deep organizational shift that takes years and lots of work to accomplish.

If you've had a persistent problem that you've been trying, but failing, to fix, the chances are pretty good that you've been trying to use a technical fix in an adaptive situation. Heifetz believes that this tendency to misdiagnose adaptive challenges as technical challenges is the single biggest failure of leadership. If we really want to change our organizations, we can't go for the quick fixes or a programmatic approach. It simply won't work. Changing the culture of our communities is an adaptive challenge that requires an adaptive leadership approach.

Manage the Pressure Cooker

Heifetz also teaches us to view our organizations and our roles within them differently. He makes the analogy of seeing our organizations as pressure cookers. Our job as leaders, then, is to monitor that pressure cooker closely—becoming acutely aware of when to turn up and turn down the pressure by adjusting the heat we apply. If there is no heat and no pressure to change and grow, nothing happens in the organization. But if the heat is too high and people are overwhelmed by too much rapid change and deep work, and we crank the heat up even higher, the whole thing could explode.

During the major redevelopment and cultural transformation that occurred at Clermont Park, the team members and residents were exposed to construction and extreme and unrelenting change for more than 5 years. We were constantly adapting and revising our operating model. We were doing deep adaptive work. It was hard and tiring. Once the final phase of construction was done, we were exhausted. I knew everyone needed a break and that applying more pressure would be disastrous. So I backed off. I turned down the heat.

Many months later, I was at a Leadership Academy gathering. We were learning about this pressure cooker concept, and someone posed this question; "When was the last time that real work and meaningful change has occurred at your community?" When I took an honest look at my community, I realized that nothing much had been happening at all.

When I got back to the community, I started to notice some interesting things. Everyone seemed extremely busy, but we weren't doing anything to move our culture change journey further along. After a flurry of incredible accomplishments, we were stuck.

I had failed to keep an eye on the pressure cooker.

Change is hard and uncomfortable. Few people will go willingly into this type of work. Everyone needs a push. Our job as leaders is to become acutely aware of the pressure cooker and adjust the heat and pressure as needed. And it's important to understand that the stronger the relationships, just like the stronger the material that makes up a pressure cooker, the more heat and pressure an organization can withstand. With weak relationships, even a little bit of pressure can cause an explosion.

Get on the Balcony

Getting a good view of what's going on in the organization requires taking a step back, or "getting on the balcony," as Heifetz would say. When we're on the dance floor, we see only what's happening in our immediate vicinity. Stepping up onto the balcony gives us a clear view of the big picture. By getting some distance we can see who's doing well, who's struggling, and what patterns are emerging. As our Leadership Academy coach explained, getting on the balcony can be as simple as pushing back from the table a bit and just watching everyone else during a meeting. By getting some distance, you start to see how people are responding to things. You notice the body language. You get a sense for when people are overwhelmed and need the heat turned down, and when they're ready for a little more heat and pressure.

Unfortunately, many of us, in misinterpreting the teachings of servant leadership, believe that good leaders are *always* on the dance floor "doing" and completely engaged in operations. And so we end up immersed in the details and unable to see the big picture. Effective leadership, especially in times of change, requires a balance of dance floor and balcony time to allow ourselves time to think, to really see what's going on in the organization, and to develop a strategy for the future.

Celebrate Incompetence

Earlier in this chapter, I told you about my experience in changing the course of that big old nursing home. I didn't start driving that change on my own. From my first week on the job, the ombudsman was relentless in driving me to eliminate the institutional framework. Each time she visited, she'd end the conversation with, "You need to go to an Eden Alternative class. It will help you. It's what this community needs."

I resisted for months, always putting it off.

Why?

Because even though I knew things needed to change, I was afraid.

I was a successful administrator, by institutional standards. I had good surveys and strong financial outcomes. I had started out knowing nothing and had worked hard to become competent in the very complex world of regulatory compliance, payer mix, and reimbursement. If I went to an Eden Alternative class, I would be admitting that my leadership approach needed to change. Worse, I would have to give up my hard-earned competence for a time because culture change was a whole new world for me. I would have to go back to being incompetent.

I've come to understand that this fear of incompetence is what drives much of the change resistance we encounter. Many times, it's the people who are very experienced and good at their jobs who push back hardest when we introduce new ideas.

To overcome that fear, I believe we must reframe incompetence. We often think of it as the ultimate insult, but accepting a period of incompetence is the only way for a person or an organization to grow. And truly, competence can be the death of innovation. The better we are at something, the longer we've been doing something, the more we identify with our roles and our expertise, the more we have to lose or give up when someone asks us to change.

When we learn a new skill, we go through the following four stages of competence[4]:

Phase 1: *Unconscious Incompetence.* Unconscious incompetence is the "how hard can it be?" phase where you are blissfully unaware of what you don't know. During this phase, people often overestimate their skills and underestimate the challenge they are accepting. This often occurs when people start in a new job or embark on an organizational change.

Phase 2: *Conscious Incompetence.* Conscious incompetence is that painful "oh, crap" phase when you realize just how challenging the skill or situation is and how little knowledge and experience you bring to the table. This can happen when people make a misstep in their new organization or fail at something new. People may feel that they're in over their heads or unable to gain the necessary skills. This can be a danger zone as people may quit that new job, or an organization may reverse course on an initiative.

Phase 3: *Conscious Competence.* In the conscious competence phase, people start to gain expertise. Things start to become easier but it's still not second nature. This phase requires continued learning and honing of skills.

Phase 4: *Unconscious Competence.* Finally, in the unconscious competence phase, the knowledge and skills have become second nature. The job or new skill can be done with little focus, almost on autopilot. This is a time when people can teach others. But it can also be a danger period, because competence is very comfortable and hard to give up. As Adam Grant shares in his book *Originals: How Non-Conformists Move the World,* experience and expertise lead people to view things in a particular way. Those who have been the most successful in the past often perform the worst in a new environment.

When I first started working on this book, I went through these phases of competence. When I submitted my proposal to the publisher, I was firmly in the unconscious incompetence phase. "How hard could it be to write a book?" I said to myself. I loved to write and I had a lot of experience and stories to tell and a lot of people I could interview.

It didn't take long to be catapulted into the conscious incompetence phase. After getting off to a quick start, my efforts stalled. Writing a book is hard! And it's different than writing when you *want* to write. It takes unbelievable discipline. And the whole process of structuring a book, properly referencing materials, and editing was new to me. For a time, I was terrified and paralyzed by my incompetence.

And in that danger zone, I almost gave up.

And then, as I was procrastinating and browsing writing sites on the Internet, I saw a quote commonly attributed to Ernest Hemingway: "The first draft of anything is shit."

And so, I wrote on the top of the page of the first draft of this book, "Really Shitty First Draft." And that set me free. Knowing that one of the most successful writers in history made mistakes during his first versions of his books gave me permission to be incompetent, to make mistakes.

I've found, when working on deep cultural transformation, that it's critical to create a culture where incompetence is celebrated. Where team members understand it's expected that they will bumble along and make mistakes in the pursuit of new skills or a new way of doing things. It's okay to make mistakes. It's okay to not have all of the answers. It's okay to have a really shitty first draft. As Suellen Beatty, CEO of Sherbrooke Community Centre, explains, transformational leaders understand that when going into unknown territory, often the path must be laid as you walk it. The leader's role is to help people take the first step, even when they don't have everything figured out.

Theory of Diffusion of Innovation

As we discussed earlier in the chapter, we must expect opposition when we introduce change. But even then, the naysayers can bring us down and make us question whether change can really happen.

I always thought that I needed to have 100 percent of my organization on board to make things happen. I spent a lot of time trying and failing to get people to adjust their thinking. That changed when I attended The Eden Alternative's Leadership Pathways to Culture Change class (based on the book by the same name by Nancy Fox). In that class, I learned a new theory and approach that shifted my thinking and released me from the tyranny of the naysayers.

Fox, and the class, introduced me to the Theory of Diffusion of Innovation, a change theory developed by Everett Rogers in 1962.[5] This theory teaches us that any time we introduce something new to an organization or a system, we can expect a standard distribution

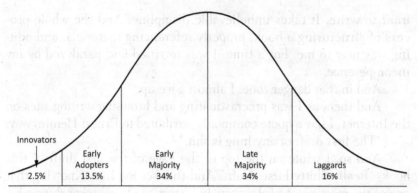

Innovators
Early
Adopters
Early
Majority
Late
Majority
Laggards
2.5%
13.5%
34%
34%
16%

Figure 9.1

of responses. People will fall into one of the five categories, as shown in the bell curve for Figure 9.1.

Innovators *(2.5 percent)*. Innovators are people who want to be the first to try something new. They're very willing to take risks. They may, in fact, be the people driving the innovation. In your organization, these will be the residents and team members who are already talking and learning about making the change or who quickly say "sign me up!" when you bring up an idea.

Early Adopters *(13.5 percent)*. Early adopters are often opinion leaders. They embrace change and new ideas but may be a little bit more selective than the innovators about what to jump on board with. The early adopters will need a little bit more information to join the journey.

Early Majority *(34 percent)*. The early majority is not necessarily averse to change. They will get on board faster than the average person, but they're likely to wait to make sure the innovation works well for the innovators and early adopters before they get on board. These people will start to move ahead when they see successes and the seeds of change starting to sprout in your organization.

Late Majority *(34 percent)*. The late majority has more skepticism about the change or new idea and will only accept the innovation when the majority of people have done so. These folks will start to move ahead when they see change spreading widely in the organization and understand that most people have started the journey.

Laggards *(16 percent)*. Laggards are generally very conservative in their approach and most comfortable with the status quo.

They will be very skeptical about the change and will be the hardest people to get on board. Generally, these folks will change only when the new idea or innovation has become the new status quo or when it is uncomfortable not to change.

There are two very powerful lessons to learn from Rogers's theory:

1. *You don't have to do it all!* No longer should you think of your role as being the one to get everyone on board. Your job is to focus on the innovators and early adopters. They will be the ones to drive change in your organization. Get them moving along and others will follow. There's a tipping point that occurs when between 10 and 25 percent of people adopt the innovation. At this point, the rest will tip much more quickly.

2. *Don't let the laggards get you down!* Usually we hear the voices of the laggards the loudest. We hear them say things like "this will never work" or "we've tried this before," and we begin to doubt ourselves and the change we're trying to enact. Expect that about 16 percent of people who live and work in your organization will think this is the worst idea ever. Know this is not only okay, but normal. Eventually they will get on board when they no longer have another choice or when it becomes uncomfortable to stay the same. Sometimes they may decide to leave the organization in search of a place that feels more comfortable.

When I teach this theory, people usually get really excited. Freeing themselves from worrying about the people who don't believe in what they're doing is exhilarating. Inevitably, though, there are people who say that the term *laggard* is a horrible word. We need to understand that laggards aren't bad people. They're just uncomfortable with a particular change. And a person can be a laggard with one type of innovation and an innovator with another type. It's okay for someone to be a laggard, except when the laggard is undermining the work you're trying to do or if you have a formal leader in a crucial position who falls into the laggard category. These situations have to be addressed. Laggard leaders will impede your progress, and usually difficult conversations must be had.

We can't allow one person to contaminate the culture we're trying to create. When implementing significant change in an organization— especially a shift in culture and focus—we need to be okay with some casualties. The first step, of course, is to work with people to help them understand the why and the how behind change and determine if their fears can be allayed.

This theory can be used to lead innovation for residents as well as team members. At Clermont Park, when we introduced to every resident the idea of new touch screen tablets for daily check-in, program schedules, and emergency communications, there was immediate backlash until we found our innovators and early adopters who would drive adoption. Remember, adaptive challenges must be addressed and worked on by the people closest to the problem. "The most inspiring way to convey a vision," says Grant, "is to outsource it to the people who are actually impacted by it."[6]

Questions for Discussion and Introspection

What persistent problems or challenges currently exist in your organization? Are they adaptive or technical challenges? How might you adapt your approach in solving them?

Are you (and is your organization) focused on applying technical solutions to problems? How could you start to employ more adaptive techniques?

What is the current culture around mistakes, failures, and incompetence? How might you create a culture where it's acceptable to be incompetent for a time while learning new skills and a new approach?

What is your current balance of dance floor and balcony time? How might you create more of a balance?

Who in your organization might fall into the innovator or early adopter category with the change you're trying to enact? How can you engage them in this work?

CHAPTER 10

Start at the Top

ONE OF THE BIG mistakes that organizations make when implementing cultural transformation strategies is to think that such changes can be driven by a single department or person, or be delegated to others by top leadership. Inevitably, these attempts result in frustration and failure as new initiatives and ideas bump up against the more traditional, institutional mindset of the rest of the organization.

The Eden Alternative, which has been educating, coaching, and consulting with organizations on culture change since the early 1990s, has found that leadership engagement and ownership are the keys to deep and sustainable change. "Culture change is a way of life, not a program," says Laura Beck, Learning and Development Guide for The Eden Alternative. "It's not about adding to what an organization is doing, it's doing what they already do, *differently.*"

In order for people to experience cultures of growth, empowerment, and community, the whole organization must be aligned with this vision. True transformation, as we learned in the last chapter, comes from an adaptive approach, where the entire organization grows and learns new ways of thinking.

Terry Rogers, president and CEO of Christian Living Communities, believes that change has to start at the top. "We think sometimes that we can just create a new building and provide training to our team members," he says. "But for transformation to really take hold, it has to start at the top. You have to shift the thinking of the entire organization and overhaul all of your systems and processes."

At Christian Living Communities, for example, the implementation of The Eden Alternative's philosophy at Clermont Park meant that individuals in all divisions, from human resources to accounting to the corporate level, were educated in the principles and philosophy of The Eden Alternative, and this philosophy was integrated into their existing operational approaches. Cultural transformation must belong to, and be modeled by, everyone—no matter what their role.

This chapter is a compilation of stories and lessons about the pitfalls of typical corporate structures and the power of integrating a new way of thinking throughout an entire organization.

Be Smart with Standardization

I was once the executive director at an assisted living community that was acquired by a huge senior living organization. Prior to the acquisition, the company that owned my building believed that the path to excellence came from hiring the right leaders and then supporting and encouraging local creativity and innovation. In fact, my regional director often told executive directors to think of their communities in an entrepreneurial way, like they were running their own small business. As a result, my team and I were empowered to continually look for ways to improve our operations.

Not long before the acquisition, my team and I had realized that we needed to better support people living with dementia and had selected training videos to watch together as a team. This wasn't one of those mandatory training initiatives where people are required to attend. Because the team members were involved in identifying the problem and finding a solution, they were excited and engaged with the learning process and how it could help them better support residents.

As we went through the training series, we began experimenting with the new theories we were learning. One of our takeaways from the training was that changing the color of plates to blue may encourage residents living with dementia to eat more because of the contrast in colors. So we tried it and studied the outcomes. As predicted, the change to blue plates led to residents eating more food. It was a huge accomplishment for our entire team, and in particular for our dining services director, Joe. That success led to a burgeoning culture of innovation. We were proud of our experiment and excited to try more new ideas.

Following the sale of the building, the executive directors and department directors from each community were called together to meet with the regional leadership team of the new company. The meeting facilitators asked for reports from the various departments at the communities. When it was Joe's turn, he stood up and proudly shared what we had been studying and the outcomes that came from changing the color of the plates.

I expected a spark of interest and excitement from our new leaders.

Instead, I watched as their brows furrowed. They exchanged looks of concern. "That's not acceptable," said one of the regionals. "White is our company standard for plates." I watched Joe's face fall. He slumped back into his chair, defeated and deflated.

I knew at that moment I would never survive, much less thrive, in that culture. That one statement spoke volumes about the priorities of this organization. Innovation was not welcome—there would be only one way of doing things.

This top-down standardization approach, which I've found to be quite common in larger organizations, doesn't impact just team members. It also sends a very clear message to residents and prospective residents about who's in charge (hint: it's not them). When my parents were exploring living options, we visited an independent and assisted living community. As we walked past the activity calendar, the salesperson explained their activities approach. "Every month our corporate office sends us the color of the month," she gushed. "This month is red, so today we're doing a class about apples!"

It was horrifying.

"Get us out of here!" my parents said as we escaped into the parking lot. "Was that a kindergarten?"

At another community, as mentioned in chapter 2, my parents attended a resident council meeting and were dismayed when every suggestion brought up by residents was met with a response from the executive director that he'd run the idea by the corporate office. My parents, like most people, are focused on retaining their autonomy and self-determination. Never in a million years could they see themselves living in a community where the corporate office dictated what they would be learning about that month based on a randomly selected color or where decisions were made by people sitting in an office in another state.

This type of culture is often driven by a desire for corporate branding and standardization. Proponents of this approach point to hotel, restaurant, and retail chains. They speak of the positive things that come from standardization. "You know what you're going to get when you walk through the door of a Courtyard by Marriott," they say.

"Every hotel has the same menu, the same beds, the same amenities." That makes sense for Marriott. I want to know that when I stay at a Courtyard that the bed will be comfortable, that I'll have coffee in my room, and that I can get the egg white frittata for breakfast in the bistro. But senior living communities *aren't* hotels. Or Walmart. Or Applebee's. As we discussed earlier, for a sense of community to develop, people need to have influence on their community and see themselves as citizens instead of consumers of services.

I understand how this sterile culture of standardization develops. I've always prided myself in being a proponent of empowerment and grassroots creativity. I worked for an organization that supported this approach when I was an executive director. But when I was promoted to vice president of operations, I found myself wanting to control things. My desire to control went beyond the things that made sense to standardize, like using the same pharmacy, group purchasing program, and clinical policies. I had to fight the urge to have all of the executive directors follow the same script for stand-up meetings and implement the same programs. When overseeing multiple communities, there's a loss of control, and fear of the consequences of losing that control can drive the desire to create consistency.

I now understand that we have to fight back against that urge, because when we operate from a place of control, we stomp the life and personality out of communities and squash the spirit of those who live and work in them.

Drive Community-Level Empowerment

The Eden Alternative, and many other models of empowerment, teach us that decisions should be made by residents, or those working closest with them. How can we drive this community-based purpose, influence, and creativity while ensuring that the culture of the larger organization is also alive and recognized at the community level?

John Cochrane has spent a lot of time evaluating this quandary. As president and CEO of HumanGood, a not-for-profit, mission-driven organization serving 9,800 residents living in 83 communities, he has a lot on the line. "The easy approach in such a large organization would be to develop a rigid list of rules and standards and scripts for everyone," says Cochrane, "but you can't control everything. If you try to, you'll never have innovation and growth."

Instead of standardizing, HumanGood is focused on creating a balance of "flexible scale with a universal personalized culture."

To that end, Cochrane and 400 HumanGood leaders from across the organization are engaged in a massive virtual book club where they explore and discuss together their culture, their brand promise, and their beliefs about aging. The goal, he says, is to create an environment where everyone understands and owns the organizational core beliefs and culture but has the freedom to interpret and express those beliefs and culture in ways that work best for each community. With this approach, Cochrane believes, the organization can ensure that all of the communities have a consistent framework and belief system while encouraging local innovation and creativity. By encouraging residents and team members to embrace the excitement of possibilities, Cochrane is finding that this approach also alleviates much of the fear that typically accompanies change initiatives.

The approach also encourages each community to develop its own identity, rather than being tied to a larger national corporate brand that is built to appeal to everyone. "When we try to become all things to all people," says Cochrane, "we become nothing to anybody."

The most successful communities in the HumanGood portfolio have the clearest identity that developed locally and organically. One community, for example, is populated mainly by retired missionaries who are focused on faith-based service to others. Another has an identity of music and social justice. Cochrane sees his leadership team's role as supporting these local identities. This means that, rather than dictating community identity, leadership must become skilled in recognizing the seeds of identity that bubble up from the passions and interests of residents and team members and in supporting and fostering those seeds so they can grow.

Terry Rogers has a similar belief that power, influence, and creativity belong at the community level. One of Rogers' first steps when coming on board at Christian Living Communities was to clarify the role of those working at the corporate office. Prior to his tenure, the organization had changed the name of the corporate office to "home office." Rogers took that one step further, renaming it the "community support office," thereby sending the clear message that the people who worked in this office were there to support, not dictate to, the communities.

Invest in Culture

When I was a kid, I went to an elementary school with an open classroom layout. The design, popular in the '60s and '70s, eliminated the physical walls between classrooms and instead featured large, open spaces. The intent was to create a new education experience where ideas and creativity would flow throughout the building. The vision for this environment was that students would work with different groups based on interest level and mastery, and teachers would act as facilitators, floating from area to area providing guidance and encouraging group learning.

Most of these classrooms failed miserably. What occurred in many open schools, including mine, was that the teachers continued to teach and function according to their old and familiar paradigm. They didn't change their thinking or their way of doing things. They simply found ways to work *around*, rather than *with*, the new open design. They created boundaries around their classrooms using bookshelves and filing cabinets and modular walls. As a result, the classrooms continued to function in an isolated manner—except they were even more dysfunctional than a traditional classroom, with kids passing notes and lobbing spitballs over the bookshelf dividers at their friends in neighboring classrooms.

This same phenomenon—of people reverting to the familiar way of doing things despite a new physical environment—is what so often occurs in senior living settings. As organizations seek to eliminate the institutional model and create a person-directed living experience, they spend millions of dollars on the construction of "home-like" amenities and features, assuming that a new building will fix the problems and eliminate the institutional mindset. Then, once the grand opening celebration is over and residents have moved in, we find people acting just as they always have.

I worked with one community that had built a beautiful new nursing home. It had small neighborhoods, cozy dining areas, and private rooms. But no work had been done on creating a different operational culture or a new way of thinking. As a result, the team was trying, and failing, to do their work in the same old way.

Like that open school, they had created an even more dysfunctional version of the institution. When I arrived on the scene more than 2 years after the building opened, staff actually said they longed for that awful old building.

Another community had spent millions of dollars to create a new rehabilitation neighborhood with a vision of a comfortable restaurant-style bistro with cooked-to-order menu items. After the building opened, however, the staff quickly reverted to the institutional system of taking resident food orders a day ahead of time. It takes time, and lots of adaptive work, to enact real change and eliminate the institutional mindset.

I've worked on a number of construction projects in my career and have always been amazed by the level of detail and focus that go into new building design and the construction process. We spend months creating space and building concepts, and poring over plans to make sure the flow of the new building will work. Once construction starts, we meet once a week with architects and construction teams. We talk about the nuances of the building and problem-solve issues that come up along the way. We track our progress and ensure that the building and all its systems will function properly when it's open.

Once the building is finished, we work through punch lists and warranty issues for months. We understand how important it is to fix problems and get things working properly—after all, millions of dollars have been invested in this building!

Rarely, however, do we employ that type of discipline in creating a new vision and a new culture or planning how people will actually work and live and function in a new space. When we fail to do this work, we find that nothing much has improved. We wind up with institutions operating in pretty buildings.

Emi Kiyota, the founder of Ibasho (introduced in chapter 7), knows the power of spending ample time preparing people, culture, and systems for success. As Kiyota says, we must first write the play and *then* build the stage. When building Ibasho Cafés, Kiyota and her team generally spend more than a year working with and preparing the people who will occupy the new space and only six months constructing a new building.

Seek Commitment, Not Compliance

Because we work in such a highly regulated field, many organizations are weighed down with restrictive rules and policies that lead to lengthy detailed missives on how to do everything. We think this sets us up for success, but what we get when we lead (or rather, manage) in this way is compliance versus commitment. In a compliance culture, we generally have people doing what we want them to do when we're around and when someone is watching. But as soon as the pressure is off, as soon as "management" isn't watching, people will go right back to their old ways.

Commitment is different. Commitment comes from people understanding the why behind the change, and believing enough in that why to work through the difficult challenges of that transformation.

Commitment means that whether leadership is there or not, whether the pressure is on or not, people will do the right thing for the right reasons.

Human resources is a compliance-driven area that many organizations overlook as they seek to shift culture. But this department sets the stage for how people will behave in the organization. The impact is far-reaching.

At one time, Christian Living Communities had a cell phone policy consistent with that employed by many other organizations. The policy forbade team members from carrying their cell phones while at work. Employees who were caught with their cell phone were subject to the organization's progressive discipline process. There was some leeway. If team members had an extreme situation, such as a family emergency, they could ask their supervisor for permission to carry their phone.

Overall, however, "The policy was extremely paternalistic and undermined individual accountability," says Jan Roth, vice president of Talent Resources. And Roth was right. As an executive director who was responsible for ensuring compliance with this policy, I felt more like an elementary school principal than the leader of a place of employment for mature adults.

Of course, the policy didn't stop people from carrying their phones. It had created a compliance culture where team members would hide their phones from their supervisor and then sneak away to use them when no one was looking. It was a constant battle. People would rat each other out for violating the rules. Supervisors would write up the offenders. And then the team members would just get better at hiding their phones. It was silly, especially in a world where phones have become an extension of ourselves and where our own organizational communication processes were becoming increasingly reliant on technology.

Worse, we weren't treating our team members like adults. We were treating them like children who needed to be monitored and controlled. And then we wondered why they behaved like people who needed monitoring.

It was clear that we needed to reevaluate this policy. We used a simple but powerful tool. We repeatedly asked the question *why* until we got to the root of the issue.

Why was this policy in place? Because we didn't want team members to have their phones with them at work.

Why don't we want staff to have their phones at work? Because we don't want them talking on their phones or texting.

Why don't we want them to talk on their phones or text? Because it's disrespectful to their co-worker and the residents, and we're worried team members on their phones may not focus on their work. It was inconsistent with our culture, mission, and vision.

And there it was. We really didn't care that people had their phones with them. It wasn't about the cell phone. What mattered was ensuring that residents, visitors, and other team members were respected and that people were focused on their work and the residents. That was the why. And that's what the policy needed to focus on.

So we changed the policy and training to focus on how it would feel to live or work in a community and be disregarded by staff who are talking or texting on their phones. We tied it into our organizational value of respect. Were there still problems? Sure. Occasionally there would be a report of someone using his or her phone in a disrespectful manner, and that was addressed. But it certainly didn't happen any more than it did in the past. And we were no longer punishing everyone for the acts of a few. There is power in calling people back to do the right thing for the right reasons. Because the organization had shifted to a culture where team members could bring their phones to work, it enabled us to implement a very successful app-based communication tool to connect desk-less workers with the rest of the team members in the organization, an innovation that has been highly successful.

Break Stuff and Question Everything

One of the ways organizations get stuck is being tied to current processes. Once we've been doing something for a long time, we get into ruts where it's almost impossible to see things in a different way. If it ain't broke, we don't fix it. To drive change in our organizations, we have to shake things up and make breaking things the new normal.

Performance Appraisals Suck

As Christian Living Communities experienced success and began to get comfortable with questioning long-standing practices like the cell phone policy, we started seeing opportunities for improvement everywhere. We started breaking things and starting over.

Our performance appraisal process was an area that dogged us for many years. We had the standard system in place. You know how it works. Once a year, a supervisor checks off numbers on a scale indicating how bad or good the employees are at their job, writes a few comments, and then has a mutually uncomfortable meeting to discuss the appraisal with each team member.

Our supervisors hated it. Our team members hated it.

One year, we were sitting in an executive team meeting discussing our upcoming performance appraisal plan. As we started reviewing the plan, Jan Roth stopped the conversation and had the guts to say what all of us were thinking.

"Performance appraisals suck," she exclaimed, "and we need to do something about it!"

We realized that our performance appraisal system was the antithesis of the culture of growth and innovation we were trying to create. If we wanted to grow and innovate, we had to focus on the same goals with our team members.

The result was what the organization now calls "gifts and growth" conversations, which focus on the talents that each team member brings to the organization, what the person wants to learn over the coming year, and what the person's ultimate growth goals are. Performance issues are handled as they should be—at the time the problem arises. Following the implementation of gifts and growth conversations, Roth credited the focus on team member growth, and ongoing performance conversations, as having played a major role in several key improvements, including a 22 percent reduction in management turnover, a 75 percent reduction in employment legal claims, and the complete elimination of complaints made through the organization's hot-line reporting system. As an added benefit, residents became so excited about the growth of team members that they doubled their donations to the organization's scholarship fund.

As an executive director, I loved the new approach and the focus on growth. I learned some amazing things about my team members—things that they had been thinking but never felt they could say out loud. My administrative assistant, for example, shared with me that she eventually wanted to run a community. She was extremely bright but didn't have any management experience and was intimidated by the financial management responsibilities of the job. After she shared this goal during her gifts and growth conversation, we spent the next two years finding opportunities for her to grow and learn in those areas. She helped me with monthly financial reviews and the budget, we gave her some departments to oversee, and she worked with all of the department directors to learn the different aspects of community management. Then, when we had a director position open up at a small community, she was prepared for that job.

Another team member told me that she didn't see herself working in the organization for long. She wanted to try something new. Because we were able to be open and honest, she could pursue opportunities that arose outside the organization without feeling guilty. And I was able to prepare for her departure. This might seem to be in opposition to a focus on retention, but as Christian Living Community's then CEO Russ DenBraber said, if we're focused on growth, that might mean we lose some people. DenBraber believed that if people left the organization feeling more confident and competent than when they joined, it was a success.

Deconstructing "Sundowning"

The folks at Beatitudes, a life plan community in Phoenix, Arizona, are also adept at questioning long-held practices. By pushing back against commonly held beliefs about people living with dementia, they've discovered something incredible—they've deconstructed sundowning, that seemingly unavoidable phenomenon in which people living with dementia experience confusion and agitation at the end of the day. Their innovation isn't a pill. Or an art therapy program. Or a sensory room. It's a new way of thinking that came from questioning the status quo of dementia services and support.

I had the opportunity to visit the Beatitudes campus to learn more about their approach. Expecting a brand-new high-tech building, I was shocked when I entered the memory support neighborhood. It's not a new building. In fact, it looks much like any memory support neighborhood. What happens inside, however, is truly inspirational. This community cares for and supports people living with dementia who have been asked to leave several other communities because of so-called behavior issues. They support the folks no one else is able to care for.

The magic of what is happening at Beatitudes is that the team just refused to accept many commonly held beliefs, including that "sundowning" is a part of life for people with dementia, that people with dementia will eventually become incontinent, and that medications are the way to fix things. They dug deeper. They broke things. They figured out how to create a true, person-directed culture for people living with dementia.

The deconstruction of sundowning came from three key realizations:

- Many of the "behaviors" that are seen with people living with dementia stem from untreated pain.

- People living with dementia don't always sleep the way that others do. They may sleep for a couple hours at a time rather than for 8 hours at night.

- Team members who would say goodbye and leave at the end of the day were triggering residents to believe that they should be leaving, too.

Based on these realizations, the Beatitudes team focuses on pain management, on helping and supporting people to sleep when they're tired and to be awake when they want to be, and on having shift change conversations and farewells take place away from resident areas.

By questioning things that many of us in the field hold to be truths, Beatitudes has eliminated the notion of sundowning. They've also virtually eliminated the use of antipsychotic medications and unnecessary incontinence. There's power in pushing back against the status quo and questioning long-held truths. What other commonly-held beliefs are keeping us from making a difference?

Find a Balanced Approach to Risk Management

My brother once worked for a company with more than ten thousand employees. He told me one day that women, whether they worked on the factory floor or in the executive suite, were forbidden to wear heels to work. The reason? One woman had fallen and sustained significant injuries while wearing heels at work. And just like that, the company forbade every employee from wearing heels. This type of knee-jerk reaction happens frequently in our field as well.

In chapter 8, we discussed surplus safety and how prevalent it is in our interactions with residents. This way of thinking also impacts organizational decision making. It's so easy to be thrown into a surplus safety, controlling mode. And nothing triggers surplus safety more than risky situations and regulations. The mere mention, for example, of HIPAA, that well-intentioned but cumbersome act that protects privacy, can cause us to lose all common sense.

During a routine HIPAA audit, our consultants flagged Clermont Park's "care line" as a problematic practice. The care line was an internal phone number residents could call to learn which of their neighbors who had agreed to share this information were in the hospital and needed prayers or support. It had been created by residents and was an important part of our community.

When we learned that our consultants recommended eliminating the line because of the risk of sharing protected health information, we went into knee-jerk reaction mode and started taking steps to dismantle it. But then we paused and evaluated both the upside and the downside risks of the care line.

When we stopped to look at all the good things that came from the care line, we realized that it was a very important means of communication and community building. It was also a resident-initiated program that served to demonstrate the importance of resident influence and decision making at the community. We realized that eliminating this communication option would disregard the wishes of the residents and would erode the community culture that we had worked so hard to build.

We realized that while it was the job of the consultant to recommend avoidance of risk, it was up to us to practice wise leadership and to handle risk in a balanced way. Working together, we found a simple solution. We added an authorization document to resident paperwork to document their choices of what they did and didn't want to share with the rest of the community. Was it absolutely fail-safe? Probably not. But it was the best and most balanced decision we could make. In the short run, it would have been easier to do what our consultant told us to do, but in the long run such a decision would have had a detrimental impact on our organizational culture. Nothing is risk free.

Dig Deeper

Kathy LeBlanc, who served as director of nursing at Clermont Park, used to say that all of us have advanced degrees from MSU. Nope, not Michigan State University. The university of Making Stuff Up. "It's human nature," LeBlanc used to say. "We see everything through our own lens and our own experiences and, when faced with a situation, we jump to conclusions and make stuff up rather than trying to figure out what's really going on."

Our organization had long been concerned about less-than-stellar scores for communication on team member satisfaction surveys. So we on the executive team set about to improve that. We purchased digital screens for the employee break rooms by which we could update the team on what was going on in the organization. We had our CEO and COO visit communities and do presentations. Yet the communication scores didn't improve. Finally, during one frustrating meeting, someone said, "Have we asked the team members what communication means to them?"

We hadn't.

When we went to our communities, we did learning circles, a method developed by Action Pact and taught by The Eden Alternative that gives everyone a voice. We discovered through the learning circles that we'd been barking up the wrong tree. When the team members were complaining about communication, they weren't talking about communication from the corporate office; rather, they were referencing communication issues between the different departments and between shifts. When we dug deeper, we were able to respond appropriately by working with the team to build communication skills and systems.

During that same period of time, we also wanted to improve recognition for team members. We purchased something called "cogs," which were triangular pieces of plastic that managers could give to team members when they did something right. In theory, they were kind of cool. The cogs had magnets on each corner and could be put together to create little sculptures. Once team members had enough cogs, they could go to a website and redeem them for gifts.

It was a complete failure.

We decided instead to go out and talk with the team members. We did learning circles and asked the team what appreciation meant to them. It turned out that they weren't looking for random gifts, and they most certainly weren't looking for aptly named tokens that truly just made them feel like a cog in the wheel.

They told us what meant the most to them was a thank you or a note from their supervisor. And even more valuable was a note or thank you from a resident. If a gift was given, they wanted something personalized that told them that their supervisor knew them as a human being.

Had we continued operating under our MSU framework, we never would have known what was important to our team members. Too often, this is how we operate. We get input from team members and residents through surveys that don't tell the whole story. And then leadership sits in a room and, based on our own perceptions, comes up with solutions and ideas that are doomed to fail.

As with residents, there are great opportunities for building community, purpose, and influence with our team members. Taking advantage of that means restructuring our meetings from one-way communication, where a leader stands in front of employees and shares information, to collaborative discussions. The right answers are out there—if we dig deeper.

A colleague of mine shared a story about being invited to speak on a panel at a senior living leadership conference. She had recently graduated from college and was joined on stage by nursing assistants and housekeepers. CEOs and other high-level leaders in the crowd asked them questions about their experiences and how more young people could be attracted to the field of senior living. Faced with a crippling staffing shortage, they wanted to hear from those they were trying desperately to attract to their organizations. I thought it sounded like a great idea, but my colleague pointed out that these CEOs came from organizations that are filled with team members just like the panelists. Why did they need to fly people to a conference and put them on a stage when those CEOs could dig deeper and just go out into their own communities and talk to the people who work for them?

Become Possibilitarians

Having led a community through a large campus redevelopment, I know the toll that construction takes on the residents and team members of a community. My community was under redevelopment for around 5 years. When that last certificate of occupancy was granted, we were exhausted. We needed to sit back and relax and not contemplate any change for a while.

During my experience as a LeadingAge Leadership Academy fellow, I had the opportunity to visit La Posada, a community in Tucson, Arizona, that had a much different approach to change. At the time of my visit to this community in 2014, they had been under construction and constant redevelopment for 27 years! Every time the community finished one project, they'd ask, "What's next? What else is possible?"

Strangely, this constant turmoil energized the community rather than causing it stress. This strength, as they see it, results from a culture that embraces change as a positive and looks at new opportunities with excitement by asking, "Why not?" La Posada leadership members describe themselves as possibilitarians—a group of people who thrive in change and chaos. The residents of the community share in this philosophy of optimism and possibility, often driving the fundraising initiatives to support the new things they want to create.

A New View of Accountability

When we explore the notion of empowering residents and team members at the community level, it makes people nervous. Some think it creates a free-for-all culture with no accountability. Terry Rogers believes this notion is terrifying to many leaders who think that their organizations will be exposed to increased risk and negative impacts on quality. "This type of culture actually increases accountability and reduces risk," says Rogers. "The people who work closest to the residents know the right things to do. We just need to empower them to do it, make sure everyone is accountable, and positive outcomes follow."

And accountability doesn't just go one way. We usually think of accountability as something that we hold our employees to. As one of my team members used to say, "We have to not only hold our team members accountable, we have to ask them to hold us accountable to the vision and culture as well."

When understanding and commitment are driven deep within the organization, team members will own the culture. At the time I was writing this book, I had begun consulting with an organization that has been engaged with person-directed care and services for a number of years. One of the key tenets of the person-directed culture is ensuring consistent, relationship-based staffing. When a newly promoted director of nursing proposed a plan to start having team members rotate to work in different neighborhoods to ensure more staffing flexibility, the nursing assistants pushed back, citing the deep relationships they had developed with residents and how those relationships created a better environment in which to work and live. They helped her to understand how her well-intentioned plan would cause them to revert to more institutional ways. She changed her mind.

Questions for Discussion and Introspection

What elements of standardization exist in your organization? In what way does standardization strengthen or harm your organizational culture?

How personally engaged are you in driving the change you want to see in the organization? How could you strengthen this engagement?

Where in your organization is there commitment to a change or a system? Where is there compliance?

When have you "made stuff up"? What opportunities do you have to dig deeper and get to the bottom of problems?

How do you (and your team) currently view change? How could you create more of a "possibilitarian" culture?

What opportunities are there to create a "break stuff" mindset?

If you were to choose one area or system to "break," what would it be and why?

CHAPTER 11

Culture from the Ground Up

UNTIL NOW, THIS BOOK has been focused on moving beyond surface-level design and cosmetic changes, instead focusing on driving a deep and sustainable transformation of culture. But what if an organization has the opportunity to build new spaces? Can architecture and design play a role in creating and supporting this transformation?

Most experts say yes. When aligned with a powerful culture, proper design can be transformational for senior living communities. As Winston Churchill once said, "We shape our buildings; thereafter they shape us." And, indeed, the structure of the spaces we inhabit can impact our emotions and our behavior.

Some buildings and spaces make us feel calm and at ease. Others make us feel alert or even nervous and uncomfortable. Interesting and complex building facades, for example, have a positive impact on well-being versus those that are simple and monotonous.[1] Rooms with soaring ceiling heights have been shown to lead inhabitants to process things in a more abstract, free manner, whereas rooms with lower ceilings lead to people focusing more on details and specifics.[2] Even the placement of furniture can impact our willingness to converse and feel comfortable with others.

In this chapter, we'll meet architects and designers and explore the impact of the physical environment on our communities. This chapter is not intended to be a guide for senior living building design. There are plenty of experts and books on that topic. Rather, it's an exploration of ideas and concepts that are sometimes overlooked, and how the built environment may support the cultures we're trying to create.

155

How Design Impacts Community

As we discussed in chapter 5, we all need to belong. That sense of community is essential to well-being. And our built environment can play a critical role in creating connections. Even something as seemingly benign as air conditioning can impact our lives and our interactions with others.

In the days before air conditioning, homes were designed to maximize cool breezes. Living areas were often situated at the front of the house where inhabitants could see the goings-on of the neighborhood. Windows and doors were flung open, creating not only cross-ventilation, but also opportunities to call out a warm "hello" to a neighbor. Large porches lined the front of most houses. It was here that families spent their evenings in the cool breezes, often chatting with neighbors who stopped as they were passing by. This structure and design encouraged residents to socialize and get to know each other.

This isn't the case in most new neighborhoods.

My husband and I live in a sealed, climate-controlled home in the suburbs. It's much like the suburban middle-class developments you'll find outside most major cities. Amenities have been carefully cultivated—groceries, fitness centers, walking trails, parks, and medical services are all readily available. Cookie-cutter homes painted in muted HOA–approved colors line the curving roadways identified by nonsensical names like Thistlebrook Circle and Wintersong Way. There aren't any large front porches here, and other than a neighbor who stands in front of his house smoking cigarettes, life doesn't happen in the front of our homes. Outdoor living takes place in tiny backyards outlined by picket fences. Frustrated by the close proximity of our neighbors, many of us have attempted some semblance of privacy by planting small trees or installing a trellis or patio curtains.

People aren't well known to each other in our neighborhood. As my husband says, it's not really even a neighborhood, it's a subdivision. There's a big difference. Interactions with our closest neighbors are limited to a nod and a wave from the car if we happen to be arriving home from work at the same time. After that quick greeting, both drivers pull into garages and immediately close the door.

Without those natural front porch socialization opportunities, the majority of communication in our subdivision comes via the community Facebook page. Every day there are new neighbor-shaming posts.

Rather than through a face-to-face discussion, residents may learn that their neighbors are upset with them about their barking dog, unruly kids, and chipping paint only by reading about it in this public online forum. Even posts from people who are trying to be helpful, for example, by warning others of coyotes in the neighborhood, spark online arguments and snarky comments. The site administrators must continually moderate the site, taking down inappropriate posts and comments.

I don't know any of my neighbors well enough to call upon them if I need help. And I certainly wouldn't notice if any of them were sick or didn't come out of their house for a few days.

One day, I was walking my dog. As I passed a bank of mailboxes, a woman called out from her car. "Excuse me, my brother just passed away unexpectedly, and I'm trying to take care of his affairs. He lived right there," she said, pointing to a nearby house. "Do you know where I would find his mailbox?" Not only did I not know where to find his mailbox, I also had no idea who her brother was—even though he lived only three houses away from me.

The people in my subdivision are, as architect, developer, and land planner Ross Chapin would say, "marooned on their own little islands in a sea of houses."[3]

Small-Scale Living in a Large-Scale World

Chapin says it's this type of disconnected and dysfunctional living situation that led him to develop a new, yet somehow familiar, housing design concept called pocket neighborhoods. In a telephone interview,[4] Chapin explained that he grew up in a small town in a neighborhood where people knew and cared about each other. There was a deep and palpable sense of community. As he began his career, Chapin realized that all too often, he and other architects were creating unhealthy environments by focusing on privacy and neglecting the design features that build community.

Seeking to remedy this social dysfunction, Chapin incorporated that neighborhood feel he knew as a child into this new concept. Pocket neighborhoods are intentional groupings of eight to twelve homes with shared outdoor community space, such as a park. They are designed, says Chapin, to create a sense of belonging and meaning and to become "small-scale communities in a large-scale world."

The limited number of households, Chapin says, is critical. If you have too few people, it's difficult to create community. People will feel that something is missing. If there are more than twelve households, there are too many inhabitants for people to become well known to each other, and the group will naturally break into smaller sub-clusters. Chapin calls this the "scale of sociability." When small groups of people are together, he explains, conversation and relationships are spontaneous. People naturally begin to share stories and become more vulnerable. The shared community space is also critical. As Chapin says, when we garden or work on a project together, we're much more likely to just talk problems through with neighbors before the situation escalates. Very livable neighborhoods can have multiple small clusters coming together in a larger aggregate community of 16 to 20, or even more, homes.

The Role of Privacy in Community

A surprising component of successful community building, Chapin says, is to provide opportunities for privacy. At first, that seems at odds with bringing people together, but Chapin explains that without privacy, community can be threatening. Rather than driving isolation, privacy actually supports engagement. "When people feel safe, and they have a place to which they can retreat as they wish," Chapin explains, "they're much more willing to be open and available to others."

To support this need for private space, each pocket neighborhood home is designed with layers of privacy that transition from the most intimate to the most public spaces. For example, a bedroom is completely private, but from the kitchen window a resident can see what's going on outside the home. If the inhabitant wants to move a little closer to others, she can open the Dutch front door and peer outside. For more engagement, she can go out on her front porch. The design of these porches is important, Chapin says. They aren't small "key fumbling" porches, but real outdoor living spaces. The porches are also designed with layers of privacy. All have railings, even if the porch is low enough that building codes don't warrant them. The railing creates an additional sense of privacy. On those railings may be pots filled with flowers. Beyond the porch is a border of plantings that provides yet another level of privacy and a transition to the larger public space. It's from this protected area that a resident can sit outside, still in a realm of privacy, and casually chat with passersby. This design provides a necessary level of privacy for those who are shy, or perhaps just not feeling gregarious on a certain day, to participate in the community from the periphery.

Somebody Who Gives a Damn

Cohousing is a community-based design concept that shares many of the same principles of pocket neighborhoods. Chuck Durrett and Kathryn McCamant brought the cohousing concept from Denmark to the United States after seeing the way that people who lived in these small, intentional communities lived between their houses instead of just inside them.[5]

Durrett and McCamant make their home in the Nevada City Cohousing community in the Sierra Nevada foothills of California. Thirty-four brightly colored, individually owned homes are situated on eleven acres of land. The homes are designed, much like those in a pocket neighborhood, to provide for layers of privacy, or what Durrett calls, "sensitive transitions from intimate to public spaces." Parking is located on the perimeter of the project. This feature is intended, like everything in cohousing, to build community. Unlike the drive-by wave-and-nod greetings in my neighborhood, the residents of this community park their cars in the exterior lot and then walk on footpaths to their homes. Along the way, they encounter other residents and may stop and chat. They pass by others sitting on their front porches and catch up on the happenings in the neighborhood.

The centerpiece of the cohousing community is the common house, which features a large, open kitchen, dining, and living area as well as a kid's playroom, a teen room, and guest rooms. The Nevada City Cohousing community also has a pool. Every home is situated so that residents have a view of the common house. Durrett believes this direct line of sight builds spontaneous opportunities for community. For example, even when no particular programs are scheduled, small groups of people will often gather in the common house in the evening. A neighbor may be doing the dishes at home after dinner. Through the kitchen window he'll see a light on in the community house and walk over to see who might be gathered there.

The cohousing model has specific guidelines for resident involvement in the design, building, and ongoing leadership and maintenance of the community. Future residents participate in extensive educational and orientation processes to ensure they are prepared to function as an effective community member once the project is complete.

Durrett explains that there is a transformation that occurs through this process in which future residents go from being complete strangers to neighbors. It's very common, he explains, that when the group first convenes, people are concerned about having as much space as possible, and even fences, between their homes. Invariably, however, he finds that when people get to know each other, they don't feel that need for fences or big separations anymore. As the project progresses, the groups work together to problem solve and make decisions such as adapting the design of their homes and common amenities to fit within budget.

Once the community is open, each resident is required to serve on the board and participate in ongoing maintenance and leadership of the community. Decisions are made through committee processes. In addition, every household is responsible for hosting a monthly dinner at the common house for any and all who want to come. I was able to participate in one of these dinners during a visit to the Nevada City Cohousing community. Some people cooked and set the table, others hung around the kitchen, chatting and watching the preparation with a glass of wine in hand. Others sat at tables and talked.

Residents of this community range from young families to older people. All of these age groups were represented at the dinner. There was a warm sense of fellowship, and it was clear that all in attendance were well known to each other.

Cohousing projects bring neighbors together in a collaborative way, Durrett explains. This leads to a lower utilization of public services, especially for older adults. Instead of an ambulance and emergency response team coming to help someone up after a fall, older residents often call a neighbor, who pops over and helps. When an older person needs a ride to a doctor appointment, a neighbor will drive. When a young working mom needs child care, a retired resident may help out. This, according to Durrett, is a far cry from what happens so often in modern society where, every time there's a winter storm or a heat wave, isolated elders die simply because they don't know their neighbors. The base concept of cohousing is pretty simple, Durrett says: It's about having "somebody next door who gives a damn" and designing buildings and spaces that support this sense of community.

Implications for Senior Living Communities

Pocket neighborhoods and cohousing are exciting alternatives for elders, but even within a traditional senior living community setting, these concepts of small-scale living, privacy, and designing for community have valuable implications.

We've seen a trend toward smaller living environments through concepts such as the Green House Project and other small household or neighborhood designs. However, these designs are still far from the norm and are usually applied only in nursing home and assisted living settings.

In an effort to create economies of scale, most senior living communities consist of large buildings or campuses that house numerous residents. And to serve all of these people, we create cavernous dining and program spaces. As a result, Chapin says, many senior living settings function as microcosms of the disconnected world that we live in.

We can borrow from the pocket neighborhood and cohousing concepts to create smaller living environments in senior living communities no matter where they exist. Pocket neighborhoods, for example, don't have to be single-family homes situated around a park. The concept of a grouping of eight to twelve households can work equally well in urban, high-rise settings where each small group can share an outdoor terrace or community room. According to Jami Mohlenkamp, principal at OZ Architecture, hallways can be designed with setbacks to allow for a "front porch" space with a place to sit and a mailbox.

We can also adapt our buildings to create more opportunities for solitude. There is a great need for this in nursing homes and assisted living communities, where privacy is a rare commodity. This is a concept that has become an area of focus for architect Bill Brummett.[6] In most skilled nursing and assisted living communities, says Brummett, the bed is usually the focal point of the room and is directly visible to passersby if the door is open. This should be the most private, intimate space, he explains. And having the bed as the focal point of a living environment, and the only place for a resident to sit, invariably labels the inhabitant as "sick." Instead, Brummett is working on new design concepts to create levels of privacy by having a seating area or table and chairs in direct view of the hallway and a more intimate setting for the bed. Mohlenkamp has been on a parallel path, designing nursing home rooms that provide privacy and a separate living space within the square footage of a typical nursing home room. In addition, when he works on household model designs, Brummett often recommends creating short hallways coming from the common space so that there is a privacy transition from the resident room to the main living area.

The creation of small neighborhoods doesn't mean that individuals live their entire lives there. Just like the residents of a pocket neighborhood or cohousing community, senior living residents also need to be a part of a larger community. This concept of a neighborhood within a larger community is often missing in household models, where the creation of spaces for larger gatherings is neglected.

As we discussed in chapter 3, cutting people off and segregating them by care needs can lead to marginalization and ostracism, both of which are extremely dangerous to well-being. To bring people together, many organizations are now building community hubs or town centers that welcome residents from all areas of living. And there are specific design concepts that can encourage this interaction to occur.

According to Rob Simonetti, architect and design director at SWBR, we can create the type of visible gathering spaces that exist in the pocket neighborhood or cohousing concepts by strategically placing small, comfortable gathering spaces along highly traveled corridors. In addition to providing a place to rest, he says, this design creates the opportunity for spontaneous gatherings to occur.

Joe Hassel, principal at Perkins Eastman, agrees with this sentiment. Hassel places amenities such as mailboxes in close proximity to gathering spaces. In senior living communities, Hassel explains, most people will go to get their mail every day. If they grab their mail and see a group of people having coffee or playing a game, they're likely to stop and sit down and chat for a bit.

Furniture selection for these areas is also very important, according to interior designer Aneka Kerlin, owner of Aneka Interiors, a boutique design firm. Kerlin pays close attention to the way that furniture impacts behavior. When Kerlin visits finished projects, team members point out areas where people just naturally and spontaneously spend time together. These spaces are usually small seating areas with a few chairs and a table, says Kerlin. "The natural way to converse," she says "is either directly across from someone or seated at an angle." As a result, sofas or chairs lined up in a row discourage interaction. Kerlin selects chairs that can be moved so people can define the distance they wish to have between themselves and others in the space. In addition, she utilizes fireplaces and background music to draw people into certain locations.

Energy Centers

We can also create small gathering areas within larger rooms. Hassel is a proponent of creating dining spaces that encourage all-day use.

His firm designs casual dining areas with features that make people want to hang out all day. Much like a contemporary coffee shop, these spaces include soft, comfortable seating areas on the periphery, perfect for people watching and conversations. They also often feature library shelves, spaces for watching sporting events, and areas that can transform from morning coffee bars into beer and wine bars in the evening.

Dennis Boggio, founder and CEO of Lantz-Boggio Architects, refers to these large, open contiguous spaces as energy centers. One of the most depressing things to Boggio is walking into a senior living community and seeing large, dark, and unused spaces. "I know something's wrong when I see that," he says.

Boggio explains that in the past, architects designed senior living communities similar to the setup of traditional private homes. This design is evident in many older senior living communities that are built with hallways from which small doorways lead to closed-off spaces. Boggio's current design practices follow the contemporary design of private homes—large, open spaces that flow into each other.

The physical entrances to spaces send a strong message, according to Boggio. Common area spaces with a small doorway and a door that can be closed sends the message that all may not be welcome. "If we want to drive inclusivity," says Boggio, "we need to create large, welcoming entrances so that everyone in the community feels that the space is theirs." This, he says, creates an environment of ownership and comfort where people naturally want to participate in community life.

I was fortunate to see Boggio's philosophy in action at Clermont Park. We worked with Boggio's firm to redevelop the entire campus and move from a segregated, institutional model to a vibrant culture of inclusivity. When you enter this community, you're greeted in a warm and comfortable town center. Not far from the concierge desk is an arrangement of comfortable seating placed around a soft ottoman in front of a fireplace. That space flows into the marketplace, a contemporary café space that is open all day. A glass wall and doorway open to a large outdoor patio featuring a pond and fountain.

The town center was designed as a hub for the entire community, where those from all of the different areas of living as well as team members and families could come together. And every day, no matter what the time, people were hanging out there. During my tenure as executive director, there would always be three or four ladies kicked back in the chairs in front of the hearth, feet (often with shoes off) propped up on the ottoman, laughing and joking. One of my favorite things during a break was to plop down on a chair with them. And I wasn't alone. Other team members and residents would walk by on their way to get a cup of coffee and would stop and chat or relax for a bit. Beyond the hearth, other residents would be sitting in the market-place reading the paper, having a late breakfast, or playing a card game. Team members were encouraged to dine in the marketplace with residents, and during nice weather everyone congregated on the patio.

Resident, team members, and family members all knew that if they were bored or lonely and wanted to just go find some people, the town center was the place to go.

In our field, too often we place emphasis on scheduled programming. We may identify boredom as an issue among residents and immediately want to add more things to the activity calendar. But real life is about more than scheduled events; it's about spontaneity. The more we can create spaces that encourage natural fellowship and fun to occur, the more we can build community and well-being.

Welcoming the Outside Community

Boggio believes strongly in creating spaces that are welcoming to outside groups. Indeed, many forward-thinking organizations are building town center spaces where local civic groups can meet and where amenities such as fitness centers, restaurants, salons, and spas are open to those from the surrounding area.

Camille Burke, COO of Christian Living Communities and Cappella Living Solutions, believes in designing communities that are welcoming and inclusive for family members and friends of residents. She has worked alongside architects to build and redevelop numerous projects. Whenever she designs new spaces, Burke keeps family members in mind. This means designing spaces where an adult child can set up a portable office for the day while visiting Mom or Dad, and having dining venues for a relaxing lunch or a quick snack. And in every building she designs, Burke includes a bistro with grab-and-go meals and a small convenience store. "What I want," she explains, "is to make life easier for the many overstretched and overstressed adult children." She understands the difficult situation in which many in the "sandwich generation" find themselves. A daughter, for example, rushes to the community from work to have a quick visit with Mom and then has to run errands and stop at the grocery store to get dinner for her hungry teenagers waiting at home. In the communities that Burke designs, that daughter can grab a healthy to-go meal to take home to her family and buy toilet paper or other things she may need. Or, if she needs a break, she can plop down in a chair at the bar and relax for a few minutes.

In addition to making adult children feel welcome, Burke is a strong believer in creating places that are comfortable and fun for kids. That means creating casual dining areas where a resident can take his grandson for a milkshake before going to the kids' room to play video games or going outside to play on the playground. To the delight of my nephews, Burke had employed many of these design features at Clermont Park. When they spent the day with me at work, my nephews said it was "the funnest place ever." And it was. Because of the intentional design of the building, they had a great day playing video games with residents and having a hotdog and a milkshake in the bistro. They ended their visit with a spontaneous squirt gun fight with their new friends on the kid-friendly patio.

A Connection with Nature

In 2016, I was in an Eden Alternative conference session led by gerontologist Sonya Barsness, who was talking about how difficult it is as a researcher to quantify the well-being of nursing home residents. "Maybe," she suggested to the crowd, "we should measure tan lines."[7]

We all laughed. But then we realized the brilliance behind her statement. One of the many sad things about institutional senior living environments is how cut off residents often are from sunshine, nature, and the outdoors.

One research study found that nursing home residents are exposed, on average, to about 9 minutes of sunlight per day compared to 90 minutes per day for younger adults.[8] Based on my experience, even 9 minutes a day seems optimistic. Looking back on my time as a nursing home and assisted living administrator, time outside just wasn't a regular occurrence in the daily life of most residents.

When people did get out, it was mostly a quick wheelchair trip from the building to the car on the way to a doctor appointment. Even in independent living settings, where people are more able to easily access the outdoors, we've created spaces where they can have all their needs met indoors, removing some of the day-to-day opportunities for exposure to sunshine. And while sitting in a patch of sunlight coming through a window might feel good, glass blocks UVB radiation, the type that stimulates vitamin D production.[9] Despite the constant barrage of information about the damaging effects of the sun, human beings do need sunlight. When we're exposed to sunlight, our bodies manufacture vitamin D to absorb calcium and promote bone growth. Vitamin D deficiencies increase our risk for health problems, such as cancer, high blood pressure, diabetes, and possible fractures.

In addition, exposure to sunlight ensures the proper functioning of our circadian rhythm, which governs sleep and wake times. Lighting manufacturers have jumped on the sunlight deficiency problem of nursing homes and have created indoor lighting to simulate sunlight. These products promise to help rebalance sleep and reduce "behaviors."[10] This technology has created a bit of buzz in our field, with some organizations investing money in retrofitting buildings with these special lights. But let's think about this for a minute—there is sunshine right outside of every nursing home and assisted living community in this country. A light that creates faux sunlight might trick the brain into thinking that it's getting sunlight, but it can't fool the soul and the spirit.

The Power of Nature

There is strong science behind the benefits of a connection to nature. Being outside in nature has been found to reduce stress, improve healing times, and improve overall well-being and health. Simply looking at nature photographs or viewing nature through a window has been shown to have beneficial effects. When you add the multisensory experiences of hearing, touching, and smelling the natural world, the benefits are multiplied.

So why don't residents get outside?

It's Too Difficult

Gary Prager, principal with Hord Coplan Macht, was one of the architects who designed a life plan community in a mountain town. It's a beautiful building in a breathtaking setting. The community is perched next to a pond that is frequented by birds and the occasional moose. It has beautiful views of the surrounding hills and mountains from nearly all areas of the building.

Wanting to understand what life was like for the residents who lived in the community's nursing home, Prager went back a few years after the building was completed and had the team admit him as a resident for 24 hours. He spent all of his waking time in a wheelchair. Prager was shocked that he was unable to get outside on his own to enjoy the mountain air and scenery. "Here I was in this community I designed in one of the most beautiful places on Earth," Prager said, "and I couldn't even get outside." Access to the outdoors required that he be able to wheel himself down long hallways, through heavy double doors, to the main area of the campus. "It was exhausting," he said. "If I were frail or ill, there's no way I would have been able to do it." The team members explained to him that they would love to have residents get outside—they just don't have time, especially when the outdoor area is far from their work space.

Prager's experience is, unfortunately, not uncommon. I had the same experience during my stints as a nursing home resident. Doorways to the outdoors are not usually visible, and if they are, the doors are often hard to open and maneuver alone. Researchers focusing on access to the outdoors have also noted that the lack of visibility and distance are major hurdles for resident access to the outdoors.

There's Too Much Risk

In her blog, Angie McAllister, Eden Alternative educator and Signature HealthCARE Director of Quality of Life and Culture Change, described a magical winter weather moment with a resident in a nursing home.[11] A big snowstorm was bearing down on the community, McAllister wrote, and Sarah Stewart, the administrator of Oakview Care and Rehabilitation Center, had gone back to the community to help. A nurse told her how excited one of the elders, Mr. Hack, was about the coming snowfall. In the middle of the night, when the freezing rain had turned to snow, Stewart went to Mr. Hack's room. She woke him and asked him if he wanted to go outside. He was shocked. And thrilled. Once outside, they talked about the experience of watching and feeling the beauty of the falling snow together. Mr. Hack commented on how the flakes felt when they hit his face. Then he threw a snowball at her.

That wonderful and cold experience shared by Stewart and Mr. Hack is usually a part of normal life. But not in institutional senior living settings. As architect Bill Brummett says, "Many people want that feeling of snow on their face or to experience being cold and retreating back inside to warmth, but instead of seeing this as part of experiencing life, we just lock the door and say it's too cold outside."

Brummett is right. Most buildings have policies and locking mechanisms to make sure residents can't go outside when the weather isn't "just right." This notion, that people should only go outside when it's a perfect 72 degrees, is ridiculous, says Dr. Bill Thomas.[12] Seasons and fluctuations in temperature are a part of life.

In addition to fears of exposure to the elements, residents are also denied the ability to go outside because team members are worried about them falling or getting hurt. I've been in communities where doors to courtyards were locked at all times because a resident had fallen and gotten injured on the courtyard. What they didn't take into account is that people fall inside all the time. This is an all too common reaction. In one study, researchers found multiple communities where doors were locked to outside areas at all times of the day.[13]

The Spaces Aren't Welcoming

Even if outdoor spaces are accessible, they're often not welcoming. Unfortunately, as we design buildings, courtyards and outdoor spaces are often an afterthought. In many communities, outdoor spaces consist of dying plants in planters and maybe a circular concrete path. We look at this aspect of a new building as simply landscaping, says Dennis Boggio. Rather, what we should be doing, he says, is to use very intentional design to create true outdoor living spaces where people want to be.

Creating a Connection

Designing buildings with easy access to nature requires intention from the very beginning. Landscape architects should have an equal seat at the design table along with architects and interior designers. Studies have found that when building inhabitants can see the outdoor area from common area spaces or the front of the building, they're much more likely to use those spaces. Too often, says Aneka Kerlin, we cover up windows with heavy draperies or position seating without taking the views outside of the room into consideration. Instead, we should bring the outdoors inside as much as possible through large windows, and address glare through sunshade-type window coverings that still allow a view to the outdoors. In resident apartment homes, Mohlenkamp recommends larger floor-to-ceiling windows, in view of the door, to bring the outside in. Even better, says Mohlenkamp, are Juliet balconies that bring a closer connection to nature.

When designing outdoor spaces for assisted living or nursing home residents, it's also important to place them in view of and in close proximity to staff work areas. My experience has been that when team members have an easy view of a courtyard or patio area, residents are much more likely to be able to access the space regularly. Designing resident service centers with large windows, and even a door opening directly to the patio or courtyard area, would help to ensure that those who may be at increased risk for falls, dehydration, or weather-related maladies can be monitored.

The design of the outdoor area also plays an important role. To allow for aging eyes to adjust to the lighting change between exterior and interior spaces, we should design for a less dramatic transition— either through a porch or overhang or brighter lighting immediately inside the doors.

Once outside, residents should have access to a variety of experiences, just as we've discussed for interior areas. Many forward-thinking developers are now creating living room–type seating with outdoor kitchens and fire pits. These larger gathering spaces are wonderful for socializing. Smaller, cozy sitting areas encourage private reflection or personal conversations.

Finally, we must be very intentional about creating doorways that can be maneuvered easily by residents who use a walker or wheelchair by adding automatic door openers. Some developers are taking this accessibility to a whole new level by creating dining and community areas with sliding walls or garage door–type openings that can create an indoor–outdoor living experience within minutes.

Back to the Basics: Designing for Independence and Purpose

As we discussed in chapter 2, there are some very real challenges that come with aging. If not addressed, these challenges can impede a resident's opportunity to participate in a community and to have purpose and independence. It's important to address these items and ensure that building design is supportive of the challenges of its inhabitants. While we follow ADA Standards for Accessible Design, there are some often overlooked design components that can help, or hinder, a resident's ability for engagement, independence, and purpose.

Vision and Hearing Challenges

My husband is a certified lighting professional. Every time he goes into a retirement community with me, he says the same thing, "Ugh, the lighting in here is terrible!" While those of us in our younger years may function just fine in dim lighting, older people often struggle. Even in our 60s, my husband explains, we need two to three times the level of ambient light as a 20 year old.

For those with low vision, lighting is critical. And, as my husband points out, this is an area where senior living communities often fall short. Aging eyes require a very sensitive transition from bright exterior daylight to more dimly lit interiors. My mom, who is living with a degenerative retinal disease, often describes how walking indoors after being in the sunlight completely blinds her until her eyes have some time to adjust. Similarly, uneven levels of lighting in hallways create dark "holes" that make it very difficult to maneuver independently. And the lack of adequate task lighting and contrast can make writing, cooking, or other activities of daily life impossible. My mom had to completely retrofit her apartment home with new lighting in order to function on her own.

In common area spaces and hallways, we should pay close attention to orienting people to their surroundings. Hansel Bauman, architect and codirector of the DeafSpace Institute at Gallaudet University, has done extensive research into adapting the built environment to support those with vision and hearing challenges. "Disorientation might seem like a minor inconvenience," he says, "but it is a major stressor and is associated with feelings of shame and failure."[14]

To counteract this, Bauman suggests having wayfinding themes throughout the building. Different colors, flooring textures, and a contrast between door frames or doors and the surrounding wall can help people maneuver. Some organizations that support people with vision loss create notches on handrails that alert persons as they walk down the hall that they're approaching an intersection. And in public and private bathrooms, toilets and sinks should be in contrasting color to the backdrop of the floor and wall.

Hearing loss also has a significant impact on our ability and desire to interact with others. Nearly half of those over the age of 75 are living with some level of hearing loss. Acoustics play an important role in maximizing the hearing that remains. Unfortunately, many of the designs currently being implemented, such as contemporary casual dining spaces with mostly hard surfaces, can make it difficult, if not impossible, for people to hear each other. Baffles can be installed on ceilings, walls, and the underside of tables and chairs to reduce reverberation.

In his work with the deaf, Bauman has learned to incorporate rounded corners in hallways. "We pick up on slight sounds as we near a corner," he says. "That sound that alerts us to someone coming from the other direction." With hearing challenges, this cue is often missing. The rounded corners reduce the likelihood of collisions.

The most important thing, says Bauman, is to include a certified and qualified lighting and acoustics engineer on every senior living project to ensure that spaces not only look good, but can also support residents who are living with hearing or vision loss to live their best lives possible.

The Design Process

Creating a Canvas

In chapter 5, we learned that one of the critical elements for creating a sense of community is to have members feel like they have a real influence on that community. Yet we have the tendency to design new senior living communities with very specific spaces to be used for very specific programs and with little to no input from the people who will inhabit these spaces.

Camille Burke, the design influencer who we learned about earlier in this chapter, has learned over the years that developers and designers should resist the urge to program the entire building. Instead, she believes in creating a canvas—spaces that have the ability to adapt to different uses and to changing preferences over time. "We build the building and create that canvas," she says. "It only becomes a community when people move into it and create a work of art on that canvas."

That work of art develops as the residents, team members, and families decide what's important to them and what they are passionate about. According to Burke, our job is to create spaces that can adapt and flow as passions change in the community. "We also have to be okay," she says, "if an area that we had envisioned being used for one thing turns into something else completely." There was a massage room in one of the communities she designed, for example. The room went relatively unused until a former radio DJ moved in and, working with residents and team members, turned that unused massage room into a radio station that has become an integral part of daily life at the community.

Involving Stakeholders

There are also opportunities to engage stakeholders in the entire process of creating a new building. Residents, families, and team members all bring different perspectives and ideas to the table that can help to ensure a building is designed to meet the needs of its future inhabitants. Paul Haack, president of Anderson Mason Dale Architects, believes that too often we make assumptions about what elders want. "We always assume they want nostalgia," Haack says. "Actually, new experiences that focus on all the senses through space, materiality, and textures address residents in a more meaningful way." By talking with residents of a nursing home about their passions, he's able to identify important ways of creating space that is grounded in real desires and rituals, such as creating customizable places within resident rooms for gardening, reading, or entertaining.

In his work at Gallaudet University, Hansel Bauman took this stakeholder input to a whole different level by ensuring that students were present not only during the inception of the project, but also during the value engineering process. Bauman explains that we often think of value engineering as a financial term—how we pare down features in the building to meet budget. In this process, however, it is truly about the "values" that an organization and its stakeholders hold themselves to. The people who will be most impacted by the new building should be involved in deciding what stays and what goes when budgets get tight. It takes more time on the front end, explains Bauman, but you end up with a much better finished product.

Sending the Right Message

The involvement and influence of residents and other stakeholders should also be clearly communicated when the building is ready to open. So often, grand opening ceremonies entail people in suits and ties—owners, architects, local dignitaries—speaking to a crowd. Some of the most powerful events I've been a part of, however, include the future members of the community—the residents and team members. During one of our grand openings, we had a proud veteran moving into the community. He and his two grandsons, also in the armed services and in uniform, performed a flag-raising ceremony for the event. There wasn't a dry eye in the place, and the resident was in his rightful place of honor. We also had a future family member speak about the importance of the new community. The ribbon cutting was done by the new executive director and her team. This sent a powerful message about who and what mattered at this community.

Questions for Discussion and Introspection

How do you think the physical design of your current community either builds or inhibits community?

What opportunities are there in your community to create "small-scale living" and layers of privacy?

How often do residents in your community get outside? What barriers currently exist to creating a closer connection with nature? How might you begin to address those barriers?

Where in your community does design adversely impact those living with hearing and vision challenges?

If you're currently planning a redevelopment or new building, what role are elders and team members playing in this process? How could engagement in the process be enhanced?

Now What?

If you take only one action after reading this book, I implore you to begin addressing ageism and ableism. We've talked about all of ageism's devastating social and economic impacts.

It is *the* most important and impactful work we can do.

If you think about all the concepts we've discussed in this book, the key mindshift that needs to occur is the way we view aging and older people. If we held different beliefs, we wouldn't have communities with segregated populations. We wouldn't have institutional practices. We wouldn't turn older people into consumers. We wouldn't bubble wrap elders in paternalistic safety practices to the point of suffocation.

We *would* have innovative cultures of purpose, possibilities, growth, and community.

One of the many challenges of writing a book is knowing when to stop. I realize that I could have included whole chapters on intergenerational living or technology or dementia or a million other things. I could have interviewed more experts and thought leaders. I could have included more research. But at some point you have to stop. And hope that you've captured enough ideas and stories to spark the beginnings of a mindshift and provide a platform for people to take these concepts further.

I worry about going back and reading this book five or ten years from now and cringing at what could by then be antiquated concepts and language. I've had to become comfortable with knowing that where I am now in my thinking and beliefs is probably not where I'll be in the future. I hopefully have many more mindshifts and "a-ha" moments ahead. If, in the future, I haven't moved beyond what I've written today, I'll be concerned. The field will continue to evolve and so, hopefully, will I.

175

I guess that's why I've shared with you so many of the mistakes I've made along the way, because this journey is all about learning and growing—personally, professionally, and organizationally.

If you and your organization are still thinking the same way and operating the same way you were even a year or two ago, alarm bells should be going off. There's no other field where push-back against the status quo, disruption, and mindshifts are more needed than in senior living.

It's so easy, though, to shut down and turn our back on concepts and ideas that aren't in alignment with our own, or to think that we have it all figured out. It's human nature to seek out team members and colleagues who think the same way we do and who confirm our beliefs. This keeps us in our current safe little bubbles of thinking.

That means we have to be intentional about seeking new and challenging ideas. A former boss used to take all of the executive directors in our organization on an annual trip to get outside of our four walls. She'd choose visits to organizations that were more advanced than we were and that were creating innovative new services and approaches. The goal of the trip wasn't for us to copy these new initiatives, it was to spark new growth and ideas and to remind us that while our communities were very successful, we couldn't become too comfortable.

There are so many ways to continue growing and learning. Reading books, watching TedTalks, listening to podcasts, and going to conferences are all great. But make sure you're not just choosing topics that confirm your current beliefs. Stretch yourself a little bit. Try exploring concepts outside of our field and then challenge yourself to see how the learning can be applied in your own world.

I once listened to a TedTalk by a scientist who, rather than relying on visual cues to evaluate the impact of deforestation, instead recorded and evaluated the sounds of the habitat. He found that while photographs showed that the habitat had rebounded from the removal of trees, the recordings of the sounds of birds and insects told a much different story of devastation and long-lasting impact.

This talk had absolutely nothing to do with senior living! But it got me thinking a bit differently and led me to start evaluating the health of the ecosystem in my community not only through my eyes, but also through my ears, by listening to the levels of conversation in the dining room, for example.

My team member, Laura Beck, often encourages people to pay attention to those new concepts and ideas that make them feel uncomfortable or "squirmy" or even angry. "Those," she says, "are the areas where you probably have the most opportunity for growth."

I hope this book has made you feel a bit "squirmy" and has inspired you to drive change. However, if there's even one little part of you that's thinking of going to your organization and saying "here's exactly what we're going to do," please stop and go back and read the book again. Remember this is adaptive work that requires everyone's involvement and engagement. It takes time and much exploration and discussion. The leader plays the important role of setting the stage for the group to begin to confront the status quo.

The most powerful thing you can do is to approach this opportunity for transformation together, as a community. I wrote this book in a way that it could be easily used in a book club format, with team members and residents reading and discussing chapters together and developing plans for next steps. Exploring topics together, section by section, can set the wheels of change in motion.

And please remember, there are organizations out there that provide support and educational resources. The Eden Alternative, for example, has helped numerous organizations around the globe achieve deep, effective, and lasting transformation.

You don't have to go it alone.

Thank you for coming on this journey with me. I wish you *not* smooth sailing, but a meaningful, challenging, and highly impactful experience—filled with fantastic failures, spectacular successes, and multiple mindshifts.

Notes

Introduction

1. Nelson, Mary Kate. "Senior Housing Penetration Predicted to Rise to 12.5% in 2025." Senior Housing News. January 22, 2018. Accessed July 21, 2018. https://seniorhousingnews.com/2018/01/21/senior-housing-penetration-predicted-to-rise-to-12-5-in-2025/.

2. Binette, Joanne and Kerri Vasold. 2018 Home and Community Preferences: A National Survey of Adults Age 18-Plus. Washington, DC: AARP Research, August 2018. https://doi.org/10.26419/res.00231.001

3. Kunkle, Fredrick. "Aging in Place Concept Has Been Oversold, Professor Argues." The Washington Post. March 05, 2015. Accessed July 11, 2018. https://www.washingtonpost.com/news/local/wp/2015/03/05/aging-in-place-concept-has-been-oversold-professor-argues/?utm_term=.9c3d47e78955.

4. Brody, Jane E. "The Surprising Effects of Loneliness on Health." The New York Times. December 11, 2017. Accessed July 29, 2018. https://www.nytimes.com/2017/12/11/well/mind/how-loneliness-affects-our-health.html.

5. Holt-Lunstad, Julianne, Timothy B. Smith, and J. Bradley Layton. "Social Relationships and Mortality Risk: A Meta-analytic Review." PLOS Medicine. July 27, 2010. Accessed July 19, 2018. http://journals.plos.org/plosmedicine/article?id=10.1371/journal.pmed.1000316.

6. "Face-to-Face Socializing More Powerful than Phone Calls, Emails in Guarding against Depression." ScienceDaily. October 5, 2015. Accessed July 15, 2018. https://www.sciencedaily.com/releases/2015/10/151005080109.htm.

7. Khosravi, Pouria, Azadeh Rezvani, and Anna Wiewiora. "The Impact of Technology on Older Adults' Social Isolation." Computers in Human Behavior. October 2016. Accessed July 15, 2018. https://www.researchgate.net/publication/303817159_The_impact_of_technology_on_older_adults'_social_isolation.

Chapter 2

1. Anderson, G. Oscar, and Colette Thayer. "Loneliness and Social Connections: A National Survey of Adults 45 and Over." Washington, DC: AARP Research. September 2018. Accessed June 19, 2019. https://www.aarp.org/research/topics/life/info-2018/loneliness-social-connections.html?CMP=RDRCT-PRI-HOMFAM-073118/.

2. Hafner, Katie. "Researchers Confront an Epidemic of Loneliness." The New York Times. September 05, 2016. Accessed July 14, 2018. https://www.nytimes.com/2016/09/06/health/lonliness-aging-health-effects.html.

3. Stein, Jorie. "Social Isolation in Residents of a Life Plan Community." Mather LifeWays Institute on Aging. June 26, 2017. Accessed July 21, 2018. https://www.matherlifewaysinstituteonaging.com/2016/09/01/all-by-myself-life-plan-community-residents-experience-social-isolation/.

4. Schoenherr, Neil. "Loneliness Found to Be High in Public Senior Housing Communities." Phys.org—News and Articles on Science and Technology. July 4, 2018. Accessed July 21, 2018. https://phys.org/news/2018-07-loneliness-high-senior-housing.html.

5. *Make Them "Feel at Home": Unlocking the Mystery Behind Very Satisfied Independent Living Customers*. Washington, DC: American Seniors Housing Association, 2014.

6. Buettner, Dan. *The Blue Zones: 9 Lessons for Living Longer from the People Who've Lived the Longest*. Washington, DC: National Geographic, 2012.

7. Landry, Roger, personal communication.

8. Thomas, William, MD. "Life's Most Dangerous Game." Performance, The Eden Alternative Conference, Westin Hotel, Atlanta, May 5, 2018.

9. Prince Follow, Dan, and David Butler. "Clarity 2007 Aging in Place in America." LinkedIn SlideShare. January 5, 2010. Accessed October 30, 2016. http://www.slideshare.net/clarityproducts/clarity-2007-aginig-in-place-in-america-2836029.

10. Hough, Andrew. "More People 'fear Losing Independence in Old Age than Death,' Survey Says." The Telegraph. February 8, 2010. Accessed July 15, 2018. https://www.telegraph.co.uk/news/health/elder/6836648/More-people-fear-losing-independence-in-old-age-than-death-survey-finds.html.

11. Landry, Roger, personal communication.

12. Rogers, Arielle, and Larissa Barber. "Why Forcing a Smile at Work Is Bad for Your Health." Psychology Today. April 26, 2016. Accessed July 21, 2018. https://www.psychologytoday.com/us/blog/the-wide-wide-world-psychology/201604/why-forcing-smile-work-is-bad-your-health.

Chapter 3

1. Tracey Gendron, E Ayn Welleford, Lynn Pelco & Barbara J. Myers (2014): Who is Likely to Commit to a Career with Older Adults?, Gerontology & Geriatrics Education, DOI: 10.1080/02701960.2014.954042

2. Levy, Becca R., PhD, Pil H. Chung, MPH, Talya Bedford, and Kristina Navrazhina. "Facebook as a Site for Negative Age Stereotypes." The Gerontologist. February 7, 2013. Accessed July 15, 2018. https://academic.oup.com/gerontologist/article/54/2/172/633579.

3. Applewhite, Ashton. "We're All Aging! Let's End Ageism." Speech, Masterpiece Living Lyceum, Philadelphia, April 4, 2018.

4. Brennan, Matt. "The Black List Unveils the Best Unproduced Screenplays of 2015 (FULL LIST)." IndieWire. December 14, 2015. Accessed July 11, 2018. https://www.indiewire.com/2015/12/the-black-list-unveils-the-best-unproduced-screenplays-of-2015-full-list-175548/.

5. Diamond, Jared. "How Society Can Grow Old Better." Lecture. March 2013. Accessed July 14, 2018. https://www.ted.com/talks/jared_diamond_how_societies_can_grow_old_better.

6. Nelson, Todd D. "Ageism: Prejudice against Our Feared Future Selves." Journal of Social Issues 61, no. 2 (2005): 208.

7. Nelson, "Ageism," 208.

8. Nelson, "Ageism," 209.

9. Palmore, Erdman. "Ageism Survey: First Findings." The Gerontologist. October 01, 2001. Accessed July 15, 2018. https://academic.oup.com/gerontologist/article/41/5/572/596570.

10. Nelson, "Ageism," 208.

11. Nelson, "Ageism," 208.

12. Diamond, "How Society Can Grow Old Better."

13. Thomas, Bill, personal communication.

14. "We Now Spend More to Fight Aging Than to Fight Disease." Next Avenue. November 6, 2012. Accessed July 11, 2018. https://www.nextavenue.org/we-now-spend-more-fight-aging-fight-disease/.

15. Whelan, David. "Boomer Bust." Forbes. July 16, 2012. Accessed July 11, 2018. https://www.forbes.com/forbes/2009/1214/investment-guide-10-aging-retirement-stocks-health-care-winners.html#5ccb843d1f9a.

16. Burling, Stacey. "Old and Ageist: Why So Many Older People Have Prejudices about Their Peers—and Themselves." The Inquirer. April 4, 2018. Accessed July 11, 2018. http://www.philly.com/philly/health/old-and-ageist-why-do-so-many-older-people-have-prejudices-about-their-peers-and-themselves-20180404.html.

17. Levy, Becca R., Martin D. Slade, Terrence E. Murphy, and Thomas M. Gill. "Association between Positive Age Stereotypes and Recovery from Disability in Older Persons." November 21, 2012. Accessed July 15, 2018. https://www.ncbi.nlm.nih.gov/pmc/articles/PMC3614078/.

18. Dionigi, Rylee A. "Stereotypes of Aging: Their Effects on the Health of Older Adults." *Journal of Geriatrics.* November 12, 2015. Accessed July 29, 2018. https://www.hindawi.com/journals/jger/2015/954027/.

19. Levy, Becca R. "Mind Matters: Cognitive and Physical Effects of Aging Self-Stereotypes." *The Journals of Gerontology: Series B* 58, no. 4 (July 1, 2003): 203–11. doi:10.1093/geronb/58.4.p203.

20. Levy, Becca R., Martin D. Slade, Suzanne R. Kunkel, and Stanislav V. Kasl. "Longevity Increased by Positive Self-Perceptions of Aging." *Journal of Personality and Social Psychology* 83, no. 2 (2002): 261–70. doi:10.1037//0022-3514.83.2.261. Accessed July 15, 2018. http://www.apa.org/pubs/journals/releases/psp-832261.pdf.

21. Mahoney, Madison. "Ageism in Health Care Found to Cost $63 Billion Annually." Yale Daily News Milgram Experiment 50 Years on Comments. November 14, 2018. Accessed November 16, 2018. https://yaledailynews.com/blog/2018/11/14/ageism-in-health-care-found-to-cost-63-billion-annually/.

22. Middleton, Marc. "Rebranding Aging® and Deprogramming the World from the Insidious Cult of Youth." Speech, Masterpiece Living Lyceum, Philadelphia, April 4, 2018.

23. "How to Dress Like a 100 Year Old Woman." WikiHow. April 19, 2018. Accessed July 11, 2018. https://www.wikihow.com/Dress-Like-a-100-Year-Old-Woman.

24. Martin, Rebekah. "Ideas for Kids to Dress Up Like Old People." LIVESTRONG.COM. June 13, 2017. Accessed July 11, 2018. https://www.livestrong.com/article/560508-ideas-for-kids-to-dress-up-like-old-people/.

25. "How to Dress Like a 100 Year Old Man." Classy Mommy. January 31, 2018. Accessed July 11, 2018. http://classymommy.com/how-to-dress-like-a-100-year-old-man/.

Chapter 4

1. Content for this chapter is adapted from Chang, Thomas, Ilana Grossman, Debbie Hedges, Nikole Jay, Alla Rubenstein, Chris Sintros, Katherine Streeter, and Jill Vitale-Aussem. "Creating Inclusivity in Aging Services." *LeadingAge Magazine.* September/October 2014.

2. Span, Paula. "An Unexpected Bingo Call: You Can't Play." *The New York Times.* February 2, 2015. Accessed July 11, 2018. https://www.nytimes.com/2015/02/03/science/a-facilitys-bingo-call-you-cant-play.html.

3. "Opinion | Mean Girls in the Retirement Home." *The New York Times.* December 21, 2017. Accessed July 11, 2018. https://www.nytimes.com/2015/01/18/opinion/sunday/mean-girls-in-the-retirement-home.html.

4. Seenichamy, Jaya, PhD. Interview by author. June 2014.

5. "Professor: Pain of Ostracism Can Be Deep, Long-lasting." Purdue University. May 10, 2011. Accessed July 15, 2018. https://www.purdue.edu/newsroom/research/2011/110510WilliamsOstracism.html.

6. Hendrick, Bill. "Rejection Affects Health." WebMD. August 2, 2010. Accessed July 29, 2018. https://www.webmd.com/balance/stress-management/news/20100802/rejection-affects-health.

7. Power, G. Allen. *Dementia beyond Disease: Enhancing Well-Being.* Baltimore, MD: Health Professions Press, 2017.

8. Power, G. Allen. Interview by author. June 2014.

9. Nelson, Todd D. "Ageism: Prejudice against Our Feared Future Selves." *Journal of Social Issues* 61, no. 2 (2005): 208.

10. Roth, Erin G., Lynn Keimig, Robert L. Rubinstein, Leslie Morgan,J. Kevin Eckert, Susan Goldman, and Amanda D. Peeples. "Baby Boomers in an Active Adult Retirement Community: Comity Interrupted." *The Gerontologist* 52, no. 2 (March 5, 2012): 189–98. doi:10.1093/geront/gnr155.

11. "Letter from Birmingham Jail." Martin Luther King, Jr. April 16, 1963.

12. Thomas, Bill, and Jude Thomas. "Ageism." Eden Alternative Webinar, February 28, 2013.

13. Landry, Roger. Interview by author. June 2014.

14. "United States Settles Disability Discrimination Case Involving Residents of a Continuing Care Retirement Community." United States Department of Justice. May 12, 2015. Accessed July 15, 2018. https://www.justice.gov/opa/pr/united-states-settles-disability-discrimination-case-involving-residents-continuing-care.

15. United States of America v. Lincolnshire Senior Care, LLC, d/b/a Sedgebrook and Life Care Services LLC (United States District Court Northern District of Illinois Eastern Division October 5, 2015). Case: 1:15-cv-08782 Document #: 3-1 Filed: 10/05/15 Page 1 of 51 PageID #:189. Accessed July 17, 2018. https://www.justice.gov/opa/file/780671/download.

Chapter 5

1. Block, Peter. *Community: The Structure of Belonging.* Oakland, CA: Berrett-Koehler Publishers, 2009.

2. Durrett, Charles. *The Senior Cohousing Handbook: A Community Approach to Independent Living.* Gabriola Island: New Society Publishers, 2009.

3. Block, Peter. *Community.*

4. Mcmillan, David W., and David M. Chavis. "Sense of Community: A Definition and Theory." *Journal of Community Psychology* 14, no. 1 (January 1986): 6–23. doi:10.1002/1520-6629(198601)14:13.0.co;2-i. Accessed July 22, 2018. http://iranarze.ir/wp-content/uploads/2015/01/Sense-of-Community.pdf.

5. Vogl, Charles. *The Art of Community: Seven Principles for Belonging.* Oakland, CA: Berrett-Koehler Publishers, a BK Currents Book, 2016.

Chapter 6

1. Strauch, Barbara. "How to Train the Aging Brain." *The New York Times.* December 29, 2009. Accessed July 22, 2018. https://www.nytimes.com/2010/01/03/education/edlife/03adult-t.html.

2. "Cognitively Stimulating Activity: Impact on Brain Health." AARP. Accessed April 20, 2019. https://www.aarp.org/health/brain-health/global-council-on-brain-health/cognitively-stimulating-activities/.

3. Thomas, Emily. "Older People's Brains May Be Slower, but Only Because They Know So Much." *The Huffington Post.* January 25, 2014. Accessed July 22, 2018. https://www.huffingtonpost.com/2014/01/22/old-people-memory-study_n_4639738.html.

4. Smith, Aaron. "Older Adults and Technology Use." Pew Research Center: Internet, Science & Tech. April 3, 2014. Accessed July 11, 2018. http://www.pewinternet.org/2014/04/03/older-adults-and-technology-use/.

5. "Clermont College of Creative Live: Lifelong Learning Flourishes at Clermont Park." *The Journal on Active Aging* (January/February 2016): 58–62.

6. Robison, Esther. "Why Does Time Seem to Speed Up with Age?" *Scientific American.* Accessed July 15, 2018. https://www.scientificamerican.com/article/why-does-time-seem-to-speed-up-with-age/.

Chapter 7

1. Boyle, Patricia A., Aron S. Buchman, Lisa L. Barnes, and David A. Bennett. "Effect of a Purpose in Life on Risk of Incident Alzheimer Disease and Mild Cognitive Impairment in Community-Dwelling Older Persons." *Archives of General Psychiatry* 67, no. 3 (2010): 304. doi:10.1001/archgenpsychiatry.2009.208.

2. Rush University Medical Center. "Having a Higher Purpose in Life Reduces Risk of Death among Older Adults." June 15, 2009. Accessed July 15, 2018. https://www.eurekalert.org/pub_releases/2009-06/rumc-hah061509.php.

3. "Have a Sense of Purpose in Life? It May Protect Your Heart." *ScienceDaily.* March 6, 2015. Accessed July 15, 2018. https://www.sciencedaily.com/releases/2015/03/150306132538.htm.

4. Navarro, Mireya. "'Poor Door' in a New York Tower Opens a Fight over Affordable Housing." *The New York Times.* August 26, 2014. Accessed July 11, 2018. https://www.nytimes.com/2014/08/27/nyregion/separate-entryways-for-new-york-condo-buyers-and-renters-create-an-affordable-housing-dilemma.html.

Chapter 8

1. Wallace, Kelly. "School Bans Balls during Recess Due to Safety Concerns." CNN. October 14, 2013. Accessed July 11, 2018. https://www.cnn.com/2013/10/09/living/parents-middle-school-bans-balls-recess/index.html.

2. Chasmar, Jessica. "Michelle Obama's 'Just Move!'–Inspired Stamps Halted Due to Safety Concerns." *The Washington Times*. October 10, 2013. Accessed July 11, 2018. https://www.washingtontimes.com/news/2013/oct/10/michelle-obama-inspired -stamps-halted-due-safety-c/.

3. Chumley, Cheryl K. "Sign of the Apocalypse: Long Island Middle School Bans Balls, Citing Student Safety." *The Washington Times*. October 08, 2013. Accessed July 11, 2018. https://www.washingtontimes.com/news/2013/oct/8/long-island-middle -school-bans-balls-citing-studen/.

4. Klein, Rebecca. "Does This Ball Ban Go Too Far?" *The Huffington Post*. October 11, 2013. Accessed July 11, 2018. https://www.huffingtonpost.com/2013 /10/08/long-island-ball-ban_n_4065353.html.

5. Power, Al. "The Hidden Restraint—Part 4—Negotiating Risk." ChangingAging. December 23, 2016. Accessed July 15, 2018. https://changingaging.org/dementia/the -hidden-restraint-part-4/.

6. Perna, Chris. "Surplus Safety . . . More Than Meets the Eye." ChangingAging. December 23, 2016. Accessed July 29, 2018. https://changingaging.org/blogstream /surplus-safety-more-than-meets-the-eye/.

7. Meehan, Mary. "Trip to the Ocean Made Nursing Home Resident's Dream Come True." Kentucky.com November 12, 2012. Accessed November 15, 2018. https://www .kentucky.com/living/health-and-medicine/article44389056.html.

Chapter 9

1. Nohria, Nitin, and Michael Beer. "Cracking the Code of Change." *Harvard Business Review*. July 13, 2015. Accessed July 15, 2018. https://hbr.org/2000/05/cracking-the -code-of-change.

2. Grant, Adam. *Originals: How Non-conformists Move the World*. New York: Penguin Publishing Group, 2017.

3. Heifetz, Ronald A. *Leadership without Easy Answers*. Cambridge, MA: Harvard University Press, 1998.

4. "Four Stages of Competence." Wikipedia. July 12, 2018. Accessed July 15, 2018. https://en.wikipedia.org/wiki/Four_stages_of_competence.

5. "Diffusion of Innovation Theory." The Theory of Planned Behavior. Accessed July 15, 2018. http://sphweb.bumc.bu.edu/otlt/MPH-Modules/SB/BehavioralChange Theories/BehavioralChangeTheories4.html.

6. Grant, Adam. *Originals*.

Chapter 11

1. Bond, Michael. "Future—the Hidden Ways That Architecture Affects How You Feel." BBC News. June 6, 2017. Accessed July 29, 2018. http://www.bbc.com/future /story/20170605-the-psychology-behind-your-citys-design.

2. Jaffe, Eric. "Why Our Brains Love High Ceilings." Fast Company. March 5, 2015. Accessed July 22, 2018. https://www.fastcompany.com/3043041/why-our-brains-love-high-ceilings.

3. Chapin, Ross. *Pocket Neighborhoods: Creating Small-Scale Community in a Large-Scale World*. Newtown, CT: Taunton Press, 2011.

4. Chapin, Ross. Interview by author. February 15, 2018.

5. Durrett, Charles. *The Senior Cohousing Handbook: A Community Approach to Independent Living*. Gabriola Island: New Society Publishers, 2009.

6. Brummett, William. Interview by author. February 14, 2018.

7. Barsness, Sonya. "Measuring the Immeasurable." Lecture, The Eden Alternative 2016 Conference, Little Rock, May 2016.

8. Noell-Waggoner, Eunice. "Lighting in Nursing Homes: The Unmet Need." International Commission on Illumination Publication: CIE 031:2006. Proceedings of the 2nd CIE Expert Symposium on Lighting and Health 2006. Accessed July 29, 2018. http://www.centerofdesign.org/pdf/LightingNursingHomeUnmetNeed.pdf.

9. "Office of Dietary Supplements—Vitamin D." NIH Office of Dietary Supplements. April 15, 2016. Accessed July 15, 2018. https://ods.od.nih.gov/factsheets/VitaminD-Consumer/.

10. "LED Lighting for Long Term Care Facilities." Walalight. Accessed July 15, 2018. https://www.walalight.com/applications/adult-living-facilities/.

11. McAllister, Angie. "The Joy of Falling Snow." LTC Revolution: Culture Change. Accessed July 15, 2018. http://blogs.ltcrevolution.com/quality-of-life/2016/01/23/the-joy-of-falling-snow/.

12. Thomas, Bill, personal communication.

13. Cutler, Lois J., and Rosalie A. Kane. "As Great as All Outdoors." *Journal of Housing for the Elderly* 19, no. 3–4 (2006): 29–48. doi:10.1300/j081v19n03_03. Doorslocked–research.AccessedJuly29,2018.http://www.hpm.umn.edu/ltcresourcecenter/research/QOL/Cutler_Kane_outdoor_space_and_QOL_2005.pdf.

14. Bauman, Hansel. Interview by author. March 27, 2018.

Index

Note: *f* indicates figures.